The Gospel of Thomas

A Catholic Understanding

Also by the author:

"Jesus, a novel"
"A Maximum Understanding of the Body of Christ"
"A Catholic Understanding of the
Near Death Experience"

The Gospel of Thomas is a collection of sayings or teachings attributed to Jesus, as told to the apostle Thomas. Half are identically or substantially alike to those of the canonical gospels. The remaining sayings are in dispute as to their origin.

The worst case estimation of the gospel of Thomas is that some of its sayings were not made by Jesus. There are only two possibilities as to the authenticity of the sayings of the Gospel of Thomas: (1) it is entirely the authentic sayings of Jesus; (2) only some of the sayings are the authentic sayings of Jesus — because so many are identical.

The author believes that all the sayings of Jesus are within the bounds of Catholic theology, and are authentic sayings of Jesus. It must be noted that not all the sayings of the Gospel of Thomas are made by Jesus; Peter and the other apostles and disciples have shared authorship in at least 22 of the sayings.

The Gospel of Thomas is self described as being the "obscure", "hidden", or "secret" sayings of Jesus, (depending on the translation). Because nearly all of the sayings of Jesus are said to two or more disciples, we must eliminate the translated word "secret". Only one saying has Jesus specifically speaking to Thomas. The prologue of the manuscript itself says that Thomas simply recorded the sayings, not that he was its directed audience. By far the most common recipients of the sayings are "disciples".

Even those readers believing that only some sayings are authentic, will gain deeper insight into the gospel based on those sayings he believes to be authentic. The gospel of Thomas is well worth the time spent studying it.

The first three manuscripts of the Gospel of Thomas were each fragments found in Oxyrhynchus, Egypt. Oxyrhynchus was a major city of Egypt and was substantially Christian (not Gnostic), until its conquest by Islam in the seventh century.

These fragments would have been parts of three previously complete Gospel of Thomas manuscripts. A complete manuscript was found at Nag Hammadi, Egypt in 1945. It was written in the ancient Egyptian Coptic language. The Nag Hammadi find was of fifty-two religious texts, mostly Gnostic.

Gnositicism was a heretical movement peaking in the second, third and fourth centuries. Gnosticism has a Supreme God, who is remote from our existence. The world was created and ruled by a lesser and antagonistic divinity, the demiurge. Christ was an emissary of the Supreme God, and speaks against the corrupt demiurge god. Knowledge (gnosis) of the Supreme God (as preached by Jesus) and of our potential to rejoin the Supreme God enables humanity to make this reunion. There are many variations of Gnosticism, and the role of Christ within it.

Early Gnosticism was not entirely at odds with Christianity. A common belief, was that our world is flawed and humanity had lost its knowledge of its true origin (God), and its true destiny (God). Gnosticism places the blame on lesser gods, who are themselves corrupt and created our corrupt world. Christianity of course, places this blame on ourselves. There are many variations within what we call Gnosticism, and even more external to these boundaries.

The author believes that the Gnostics attached themselves (and their interpretation) to the genuine gospel of Jesus, which we now call "the Gospel of Thomas", rather than writing it. The Gospel of Thomas was also widely used within the mainstream Christian Church, and most manuscripts have been found in these Christian churches.

The date of origin of the Gospel of Thomas is unknown and disputed. Many estimates of its recording as a manuscript place it as early as the canonical gospels. Many of the sayings are virtually identical to those in the canonical gospels, and must have their origin in Jesus.

It does appear that the Gospel of Thomas is an independent and parallel gospel. Its teachings do not appear to be copied from the canonical gospels. The evidence for this is that many teachings are worded the same, while others are the same in substance but with a different wording. If the canonical gospels were simply copied into Thomas, all the wording would be the same.

Different wording for the same teaching occurs between the four canonical gospels, as it does in the Gospel of Thomas. Like the canonical gospels, the Gospel of Thomas has existed in Greek, Coptic, and Syrian languages. The only known complete manuscript is in the Egyptian Coptic language.

The following is the Gospel of Thomas, (combined Greek and Coptic translations) with relevant explanations of the sayings according to Catholic theology:

These are the obscure sayings that the living Jesus spoke and Didymos Judas Thomas recorded.

This prologue has several interpretations, with the world obscure sometimes translated into: "hidden", or "secret". "Secret" is an unlikely meaning since the sayings usually have Jesus speaking to two or more disciples, or a crowd of listeners.

The following Gospel of Thomas sayings (logoi) are primarily from the English translations of the Egyptian Coptic language manuscript. Where brackets [ ] occur, it indicates a word that is missing due to manuscript damage [...], or damaged but estimated by scholars, [word].

1. And he said, "Whoever discovers the interpretation of these sayings will not taste death."

This is similar to Jn 8:51, "Very truly, I tell you, whoever keeps my word will never see death.". The original manuscripts do not number the sayings.

This saying in no way challenges Christian dogma, but the word "interpretation", would appeal to the Gnostics, as some sort of secret knowledge. The Christian would "interpret" the words of Jesus into personal actions.

2. Jesus said, "Those who seek should not stop seeking until they find. When they find, they will be disturbed. When they are disturbed, they will marvel, and will reign over all."

Catholic teaching is that we become members of the body of Christ, we literally become Christ (CCC 1213, 790, 795), who is now: Jesus, Eucharist and the faithful. The first reaction to this idea is disturbance or disbelief, then marvel, then a sharing in the very life and reign of God. See the appendix for details of the Catholic understanding of the body of Christ.

3. Jesus said, "If your leaders say to you, 'Look, the Father's kingdom is in the sky,' then the birds of the sky will precede you. If they say to you, 'It is in the sea,' then the fish will precede you. Rather, the Father's kingdom is within you and it is outside you."

"When you know yourselves, then you will be known, and you will understand that you are children of the living Father. But if you do not know yourselves, then you live in poverty, and you are the poverty."

The first half is similar to Lk 17:20-21, "Once Jesus was asked by the Pharisees when the kingdom of God was coming, and he answered, "The kingdom of God is not coming with things that can be observed; nor will they say, 'Look, here it is!' or 'There it is!'; for, in fact, the kingdom of God is among you."

The second paragraph calls us know or realize that we are children of God; such knowledge is implied belief in God, which even alone can lead to our salvation by Christ. *If we fail to know, hope and ask, then we remain in and as poverty, rather than in our intended fulfilled state.*

In Mt 7:23 Jesus says, "And then I will declare to them, '<u>I never knew you</u>; depart from me, you who practice lawlessness!'"[1] *St. Thomas Aquinas spoke of knowledge as a sort of participation in the object known. When we think of a*

---

[1] In both the canonical gospels and the Gospel of Thomas, several teachings link knowledge of Christ to salvation, this idea may have been the core around which Gnosticism was formed. We observe however that knowledge of Christ was not enough to attain salvation for the fallen angels (for example). Inclination of the will toward Christ, or at least toward virtue is required.

The Gnostics strayed more significantly in that they did not subscribe to the sacraments, they believed Christ to be simply a higher order semi-god, and they saw the material world as inherently evil.

tree, we become in part, the tree. We share in the idea of a tree. We do not have the ability to fully become the tree, because of our God given limitations.

By God's grace we may fully become Christ, who is now the entire body of Christ. Christ's act of knowledge or participation in us, includes us into his person. There is more to it than knowledge of course, but this specific teaching in Thomas is contained within the bounds of Catholic theology.

4. Jesus said, "The person old in days won't hesitate to ask a little child seven days old about the place of life, and that person will live."

"For many of the first will be last, and will become a single one."

The child is among the least of persons, yet he may end up as the first. This is because of the child's depth of participation in Christ. If not by his understanding then by his action. The "person old in days", does well to consult the child. There does seem to be some literary exaggeration in this teaching, and Jesus often made such rhetorical exaggeration.

5. Jesus said, "Know what is in front of your face, and what is hidden from you will be disclosed to you."

"For there is nothing hidden that will not be revealed. And there is nothing buried that will not be raised."

What is in front of the listener's face is Jesus. When we know or participate in Jesus, the larger world of Christ is disclosed to us. We could translate the word "know" into the word "believe", and arrive at the same meaning. The last sentence of the teaching appears in the Greek manuscript, but not in the Coptic. The Coptic Thomas is far more complete and forms the bulk of the English translation.

6. His disciples asked him and said to him, "Do you want us to fast? How should we pray? Should we give to charity? What diet should we observe?" [2]

Jesus said, "Don't lie, and don't do what you hate, because all things are disclosed before heaven. After all, there is nothing hidden that will not be revealed, and there is nothing covered up that will remain undisclosed."

The disciples are asking about religious protocol, which is secondary to moral substance.

In the second paragraph, Jesus then explains the more vital elements of religion, "Don't do what you hate.", translates to "Don't do what you hate in your moral conscious.".

This saying is similar to Lk 8:17, "For there is nothing hidden that will not be disclosed, and nothing concealed that will not be known or brought out into the open."

7. Jesus said, "Lucky is the lion that the human will eat, so that the lion becomes human. And foul is the human that the lion will eat, and the lion still will become human."

Because a teaching is mystical and abstruse does not make it inauthentic or erroneous. A possible explanation is as follows: the lion is consumed and becomes the man who has the good fortune of being a member of Christ, (the body of Christ). The foul human is someone distant from Christ, and the lion that is consumed enjoys no real increase in stature. This teaching uses figurative language to promote one's inclusion into the body of Christ.

---

[2] Strictly speaking, the first half of saying 6 is spoken by the disciples, not Jesus. Other sayings of shared authorship are: 12, 13, 18, 20, 21, 22, 24, 37, 43, 51, 52, 53, 60, 61, 72, 79, 91, 99, 100, 104, 113, 114.

8. And he said, "The person is like a wise fisherman who casts his net into the sea and drew it up from the sea full of little fish. Among them the wise fisherman discovered a fine large fish. He threw all the little fish back into the sea, and easily chose the large fish. Anyone here with two good ears had better listen!"

This is identical in meaning to Mt 13:47-48, and similar to the pearl of great price (Mt 13:45-46), or the field of treasure (Mt 13:44).

9. Jesus said, "Look, the sower went out, took a handful of seeds, and scattered them. Some fell on the road, and the birds came and gathered them. Others fell on rock, and they didn't take root in the soil and didn't produce heads of grain. Others fell on thorns, and they choked the seeds and worms ate them. And others fell on good soil, and it produced a good crop: it yielded sixty per measure and one hundred twenty per measure."

This is virtually identical in wording to the parable of the sower, Mt 13:1-9. This is an example of a Gospel of Thomas saying that could only have its origin with Jesus. Many such sayings in the Gospel of Thomas are identical in word or meaning to the canonical gospels, and can only have Jesus as the author. [3]

---

[3] The canonical gospels are guaranteed to be free of moral or theological error. At least two non-canonical teaching documents of the early Church, the Didache and the Shepard of Hermas, are used in the Catechism as official teaching. Pope Benedict XVI has quoted from the Gospel of Thomas. Non-canonical documents may or may not be free of error, they are simply not guaranteed. Within the canonical gospels a person may make both morally correct and incorrect acts, this occurred with both Judas and Peter, and any human for that matter.

10. Jesus said, "I have cast fire upon the world, and look, I'm guarding it until it blazes."

This is a different wording of Lk 12:49. The fire is usually thought to be the Holy Spirit.

11. Jesus said, "This heaven will pass away, and the one above it will pass away."

"The dead are not alive, and the living will not die. During the days when you ate what is dead, you made it come alive. When you are in the light, what will you do? On the day when you were one, you became two. But when you become two, what will you do?"

From Mt 24:35, "Heaven and earth will pass away, but my words will not pass away."; also Mk 13:31, Lk 16:17, 21:33; 2 Pet 3:10.

As to the second part, the only real new teaching is "On the day when you were one, you became two. But when you become two, what will you do?". We have our origin in Christ, we were once an idea internal to Christ, we were then incarnated as persons distinct from Christ, and our intended destiny is to rejoin Christ as members of the body of Christ, (CCC 398). Our creation involves one becoming two (Christ creates us; there then exists Christ and his creation). What then shall we do after our creation...follow Christ to our intended reunion.

12. The disciples said to Jesus, "We know that you are going to leave us. Who will be our leader?"

Jesus said to them, "No matter where you are you are to go to James the Just, for whose sake heaven and earth came into being."

This is a sound bite, of which we do not know the surrounding facts. It is sometimes seen as a denial of Peter as the first leader. Several valid scenarios are possible which retain Peter as Pope, and James as a leader in the early Church:

(1) The time is post resurrection and Jesus appears to some disciples, as he does in the canonical gospels. These disciples (not apostles) are within the jurisdiction of the bishop of Jerusalem (who is historically James the Just), and are simply told to obey their bishop, to who Jesus has delegated authority.

(2) Post resurrection again, Peter has been arrested and incommunicado. By prior decision of Peter, leadership reverts to James if Peter is unable to lead.

(3) Again, post resurrection Jesus is talking to some unknown number of disciples, who may or may not be apostles. He may be talking to half of the apostles and telling them to place themselves under the leadership of James, because Peter has split Christendom into the area west of Jerusalem, (lead by Peter), and the area east of Jerusalem (lead by James), with both areas under the ultimate leadership of Peter. This scenario meshes exactly with the gospel account in Acts 15, where James, the bishop of Jerusalem, takes local command.

This saying in Thomas does seem to have Jesus in a post resurrection appearance. It is unlikely that Peter or James made large scale leading while Jesus was alive.

The Acts of the Apostles does show Peter delegating much authority to James at the council of Jerusalem, (Acts 15). Two things are known of Peter's papacy: (1) he was the first Pope; (2) at some point his papacy was terminated because of death, health or decision. It is possible that James was Pope at some point after Peter, although the three scenarios proposed retain James as bishop of Jerusalem, and any other areas or responsibilities designated by Peter.

There is much more unknown about the structure of the early church than is known. It is possible that Peter tasked the capable James with development of doctrine (this is James' function in Acts 15), with Peter as the ultimate overseer. Peter seems to have delegated such authority to James at the council of Jerusalem in Acts 15.

13. Jesus said to his disciples, "Compare me to something and tell me what I am like."

Simon Peter said to him, "You are like a just messenger."

Matthew said to him, "You are like a wise philosopher."

Thomas said to him, "Teacher, my mouth is utterly unable to say what you are like."

Jesus said, "I am not your teacher. Because you have drunk, you have become intoxicated from the bubbling spring that I have tended."

"And he took him, and withdrew, and spoke three sayings to him. When Thomas came back to his friends they asked him, "What did Jesus say to you?"

"Thomas said to them, "If I tell you one of the sayings he spoke to me, you will pick up rocks and stone me, and fire will come from the rocks and devour you."

In the fifth paragraph, Jesus teaches that his disciples must deny themselves (deny their self interest). The disciples do not follow this teaching, but rather become spiritually intoxicated, or disciples only of the joyful parts of Christianity, (therefore Jesus is not really their teacher).

Regarding the seventh paragraph, many people wanted to stone Jesus during his career, his teachings were radical and interpreted to be in opposition to the Jewish faith.

14. Jesus said to them, "If you fast, you will bring sin upon yourselves, and if you pray, you will be condemned, and if you give to charity, you will harm your spirits."

"When you go into any region and walk about in the countryside, when people take you in, eat what they serve you and heal the sick among them."

"After all, what goes into your mouth will not defile you; rather, it's what comes out of your mouth that will defile you."

Regarding the first astounding paragraph, there is only one person who could speak it with authority...Jesus. This is the same Jesus who said, "you must hate your father, your mother, and even your own life", (Lk 14:26). This is the same Jesus who said, "Whoever eats my flesh and drinks my blood has eternal life...", (Jn 6:54). This is the same Jesus who said, "Woe to you who are filled or happy, for you will be hungry and weeping.", (Lk 6:25).

If these canonical teachings appeared only in the Gospel of Thomas, they would be declared fraudulent, but Jesus <u>did</u> say *them. Jesus is also the author of this strange teaching in the Gospel of Thomas, and it has the same sound foundation as his canonical demand that we hate father, mother and our own lives.*

Our salvation is to become Christ (who is now the entire body of Christ, see also footnote 8, page 74). We many not become Christ if we remain self (hence, we must hate our lives). We may not ascend to God if we remain attached to: father, mother, riches, status, pleasure or misery, or even the Law of Moses.

Strictly speaking, to make these things (fasting, prayer, almsgiving) our end, is failure to achieve our true end, which is a sharing in Christ, who is now the body of Christ. The Pharisees were famous for concentrating on religious ritual at the expense of religious substance. The Law of Moses was their end, rather than the Messiah among them.

In the first paragraph, Jesus may be speaking to some Pharisees who see prayer, fasting and alms giving in the Law of Moses as the final end of religion. Jesus uses the fist of rhetorical exaggeration to demolish this error, then rebuild.

Again in the second and third paragraphs we see teachings that are identical to canonical verses.

15. Jesus said, "When you see one who was not born of woman, fall on your faces and worship. That one is your Father."

Self explanatory: when we see the Father (in Heaven presumably), we give worship.

16. Jesus said, "Perhaps people think that I have come to cast peace upon the world. They do not know that I have come to cast conflicts upon the earth: fire, sword, war."

"For there will be five in a house: there'll be three against two and two against three, father against son and son against father, and they will stand alone."

From Mt 10:34-36, "Do not think that I have come to bring peace to the earth; I have not come to bring peace, but a sword. For I have come to set a man against his father, and a daughter against her mother, and a daughter-in-law against her mother-in-law, and one's foes will be members of one's own household."

17. Jesus said, "I will give you what no eye has seen, what no ear has heard, what no hand has touched, what has not arisen in the human heart."

Jesus is retelling Isaiah 64:4.

18. The disciples said to Jesus, "Tell us, how will our end come?"

Jesus said, "Have you found the beginning, then, that you are looking for the end? You see, the end will be where the beginning is."

"Congratulations to the one who stands at the beginning: that one will know the end and will not taste death."

Rev 22:13, "I am the Alpha and the Omega, the First and the Last, the Beginning and the End." Jesus says that the one who stands at the beginning knows the end, and will not taste death. We have our beginning as an idea within Christ, we are created as humans and our intended destiny or end is to rejoin Christ as part of his larger body of Christ.

One idea as to why Christ creates us, is that we increase our ability to love by the challenges of a fallen world. We then bring our spiritual advancement to the body of Christ. God, who cannot increase in love, has found a way to do just that.

19. Jesus said, "Congratulations to the one who came into being before coming into being."

"If you become my disciples and pay attention to my sayings, these stones will serve you."

"For there are five trees in Paradise for you; they do not change, summer or winter, and their leaves do not fall. Whoever knows them will not taste death."

The one who came into being before coming into being is Jesus Christ, (and mystically, all who share in Jesus, in the body of Christ). Trinitarian Son of God (Christ) existed before the creation of human Jesus. Jesus was fully human and fully God, he had a created human nature, and an uncreated divine nature.

Jesus is not really congratulating himself, but those who will join him in the body of Christ. Some translators replace "Congratulations to", with "Blessed is"; it makes more sense that Jesus would say this of his disciples, rather than himself.

The second paragraph simply observes that Christ, who is now the entire body of Christ, even has the stones of the earth at his service. Our entry into the body of Christ is in substantial part by following the teachings of Christ.

The five trees of Heaven are not mentioned anywhere in the bible or Jewish or Christian tradition, but such mysticism is not at odds with any dogma. It is difficult to see how this saying promotes the specific cause of Gnosticism, and it is likely from Jesus, and not the Gnostics.

20. The disciples said to Jesus, "Tell us what Heaven's kingdom is like."

He said to them, "It's like a mustard seed, the smallest of all seeds, but when it falls on prepared soil, it produces a large plant and becomes a shelter for birds of the sky."

Another saying identical in meaning to the canonical gospel; Mt 13:31-32, Mk 4:30-32, Lk 13:18-19.

21. Mary said to Jesus, "What are your disciples like?"

He said, "They are like little children living in a field that is not theirs. When the owners of the field come, they will say, 'Give us back our field.' They take off their clothes in front of them in order to give it back to them, and they return their field to them."

"For this reason I say, if the owners of a house know that a thief is coming, they will be on guard before the thief arrives and will not let the thief break into their house and steal their possessions."

"As for you, then, be on guard against the world. Prepare yourselves with great strength, so the robbers can't find a way to get to you, for the trouble you expect will come."

"Let there be among you a person who understands."

"When the crop ripened, he came quickly carrying a sickle and harvested it. Anyone here with two good ears had better listen!"

The second paragraph has the disciples returning this world (so to speak) back to "the ruler of this world", who is the Devil, (Jn 12:31). The theology is not to cling to the things of this world or life, since it is not really part of the kingdom of God. The disciples (termed children), withhold nothing (of this world), and even return their clothing.

The third and fourth paragraphs have the robber-Devils and even an unwitting world attempting to steal what really belongs to us, one's soul. Jesus advises the listener to be aware of this, and be on guard.

22. Jesus saw some babies nursing. He said to his disciples, "These nursing babies are like those who enter the Father's kingdom."

They said to him, "Then shall we enter the Father's kingdom as babies?"

Jesus said to them, "When you make the two into one, and when you make the inner like the outer and the outer like the inner, and the upper like the lower, and when you make male and female into a single one, so that the male will not be male nor the female be female, when you make eyes in place of an eye, a hand in place of a hand, a foot in place of a foot, an image in place of an image, then you will enter the kingdom."

An ideal infant is totally dependent, committed and appreciative of his mother who nurtures him, that's all that Jesus asks of us.

The last paragraph has two (Jesus and disciple) becoming one in the body of Christ, who is the single person of Christ. The body of Christ has individual members, who lose none of their human senses or abilities, but gain a share in the divinity and person of Christ. We would call it a person made of persons, but there is only one person, that of Christ. In this life we join the human nature of Christ, then later in Heaven we join the divine nature of Christ.

Since the body of Christ is made of millions of human individuals, it cannot be said to be either male or female, not to mention its angelic and Eucharistic members. See the author's book, "A Maximum Understanding of the Body of Christ", for detailed explanations of every aspect of the body of Christ: angels, humans, Eucharist. It is a free online read at www.free-ebooks.net.

23. Jesus said, "I shall choose you, one from a thousand and two from ten thousand, and they will stand as a single one."

Again, Christ is now the single person we call the body of Christ, who is made of many members.

24. His disciples said, "Show us the place where you are, for we must seek it."

He said to them, "Anyone here with two ears had better listen! There is light within a person of light, and it shines on the whole world. If it does not shine, it is dark."

The disciples want to see the place called Heaven, but Heaven is the person of Jesus Christ. The light of Heaven is contained within a person, rather than a place we travel to. We recall that Jesus tells us he is the literal resurrection, (Jn 11:25). So too is Jesus our literal Heaven.

25. Jesus said, "Love your friends like your own soul, protect them like the pupil of your eye."

Love yourself, others and God. That's unconditional love — everyone, every time, every situation.

26. Jesus said, "You see the sliver in your friend's eye, but you don't see the timber in your own eye. When you take the timber out of your own eye, then you will see well enough to remove the sliver from your friend's eye."

Mt7:3-5, Lk 6:41-42. As stated earlier, with so many Gospel of Thomas sayings nearly identical to the canonical gospels, many or most are certainly from Jesus. Worst case for the Gospel of Thomas is that some sayings are forgeries, and most are authentic.

27. "If you do not fast from the world, you will not find the Father's kingdom. If you do not observe the Sabbath as a Sabbath you will not see the Father."

This is an example of a saying with no canonical parallel, but is entirely within the bounds of Catholic teaching.

28. Jesus said, "I took my stand in the midst of the world, and in flesh I appeared to them. I found them all drunk, and I did not find any of them thirsty. My soul ached for the children of humanity, because they are blind in their hearts and do not see, for they came into the world empty, and they also seek to depart from the world empty."

"But meanwhile they are drunk. When they shake off their wine, then they will change their ways."

Jesus might have said, "My children come into the world empty, (because of original sin, which infects us as we enter into creation), and they also seek to depart from the world empty." This is a sad and profound teaching of Jesus Christ.

This saying (and others) reveal a belief common to Christianity and Gnosticism , (and almost any religion) — that we lack a proper knowledge of our condition, and that we are called to a life superior than the one which we now live.

The Christian view is that this better life is an actual sharing in the life of Christ (CCC 398). The many forms of Gnosticism have Jesus as a prophet, or a semi-god who has himself attained freedom from corruption, but is not a savior.

29. Jesus said, "If the flesh came into being because of spirit, that is a marvel, but if spirit came into being because of the body, that is a marvel of marvels."

"Yet I marvel at how this great wealth has come to dwell in this poverty."

"Flesh coming into being because of spirit", refers to the creation of humanity, from God who is a spirit. The "spirit coming into being because of a body", is Jesus. The Trinitarian Son of God took on a created nature (came into being), due to his taking a bodily human nature. Jesus then comments that our fallen world and persons are the very poverty that Jesus Christ must dwell amongst.

30. Jesus said, "Where there are three deities, they are divine. Where there are two or one, I am with that one."

The three deities are the Trinity, which is in fact three divine persons constituting one God. The second sentence is from Mt 18:20; "For where two or three are gathered in my name, I am there among them."

31. Jesus said, "No prophet is welcome on his home turf; doctors don't cure those who know them."

From Mk 6:4, "Then Jesus said to them, 'Prophets are not without honor, except in their hometown, and among their own kin, and in their own house.'"

32. Jesus said, "A city built on a high hill and fortified cannot fall, nor can it be hidden."

From Mt 5:14 "You are the light of the world. A city built on a hill cannot be hid."

33. Jesus said, "What you will hear in your ear, in the other ear proclaim from your rooftops."

"After all, no one lights a lamp and puts it under a basket, nor does one put it in a hidden place. Rather, one

puts it on a lampstand so that all who come and go will see its light."

From Mt 10:27, "What I say to you in the dark, tell in the light; and what you hear whispered, proclaim from the housetops."

From Lk 8:16, "No one after lighting a lamp hides it under a jar, or puts it under a bed, but puts it on a lamp stand, so that those who enter may see the light."

The first paragraph is an idiom, telling a person to relay a message. We hear from the side, and turn to the other side to repeat it, and the other ear then hears the message as well.

34. Jesus said, "If a blind person leads a blind person, both of them will fall into a hole."

Mt 15:14, "Let them alone; they are blind guides of the blind. And if one blind person guides another, both will fall into a pit."

35. Jesus said, "One can't enter a strong person's house and take it by force without tying his hands. Then one can loot his house."

Mk 3:27, "But no one can enter a strong man's house and plunder his property without first tying up the strong man; then indeed the house can be plundered." The strong man is the Devil of course, who Jesus says is the ruler of this world, (Jn 12:31). If his evil is remediated into virtue (by Jesus and the ongoing body of Christ), then his power is taken away.

36. Jesus said, "Do not fret, from morning to evening and from evening to morning about your food, what you're going to eat, or about your clothing, what you are going to wear. You're much better than the lilies, which neither card nor spin."

"As for you, when you have no garment, what will you put on? Who might add to your stature? That very one will give you your garment."

From Mt 6:25-29, "Therefore I tell you, do not worry about your life, what you will eat or what you will drink, or about your body, what you will wear. Is not life more than food, and the body more than clothing? Look at the birds of the air; they neither sow nor reap nor gather into barns, and yet your heavenly Father feeds them. Are you not of more value than they? And can any of you by worrying add a single hour to your span of life? And why do you worry about clothing? Consider the lilies of the field, how they grow; they neither toil nor spin, yet I tell you, even Solomon in all his glory was not clothed like one of these."

37. His disciples said, "When will you appear to us, and when will we see you?"

Jesus said, "When you strip without being ashamed, and you take your clothes and put them under your feet like little children and trample them, then [you] will see the son of the living one and you will not be afraid."

Selflessness is a core element of Christianity, we cannot become Christ if we remain committed to self, self interest, and in this case self pride. This is a bit different than the children giving back their clothes in saying 21. Here the conquest of self shame in necessary. Nakedness is of course not a Christian requirement but a semi-rhetorical moral example, made by the great preacher Jesus.

This idea of denial of self appearing in the second paragraph explains the first paragraph. We shall "see" Christ, as we make greater sharing in him, by denying self, and cultivating Christ.

38. Jesus said, "Often you have desired to hear these sayings that I am speaking to you, and you have no one

else from whom to hear them. There will be days when you will seek me and you will not find me."

From Luke 10:24, "...for I tell you, that many prophets and kings have desired to see those things which ye see.". See also: Luke 17:22, Matt 13:10-17, John 7:32-36.

39. Jesus said, "The Pharisees and the scholars have taken the keys of knowledge and have hidden them. They have not entered nor have they allowed those who want to enter to do so."

"As for you, be as sly as snakes and as simple as doves."

From Mt 23:13, "Woe to you, scribes and Pharisees, you hypocrites. You lock the kingdom of heaven before men. You do not enter yourselves, nor do you allow entrance to those trying to enter."

From Mt 10:16, "See, I am sending you out like sheep into the midst of wolves; so be wise as serpents and innocent as doves."

40. Jesus said, "A grapevine has been planted apart from the Father. Since it is not strong, it will be pulled up by its root and will perish."

From Mt 15:13, "He answered, 'Every plant that my heavenly Father has not planted will be uprooted.'"

41. Jesus said, "Whoever has something in hand will be given more, and whoever has nothing will be deprived of even the little they have."

Mt 25:29, "To all those who have, more will be given, and they will have an abundance; but from those who have nothing, even what they have will be taken away." Our initial participation in the body of Christ is in the human

Jesus, and we have a certain attainment of grace, (even those distant from God enjoy his gifts).

At judgment Christ (who is God), attempts communion of us into his divine nature (CCC 398). When we make it, we then share in the entire divine Christ. Purgatory of course would be a delay.

Judgment is really the communion that Jesus designed for us from the beginning (CCC 398). In this final communion Jesus takes all goodness into himself. Any evil and those owning it cannot make the union and are left behind, devoid of any previous goodness. This evil left behind is Hell. See also the appendix on Hell.

42. Jesus said, "Be passersby."

It is an often appearing idea in the canonical gospels, that we should not cling to the things of this life or world.

43. His disciples said to him, "Who are you to say these things to us?"

"You don't understand who I am from what I say to you."

"Rather, you have become like the Judeans, for they love the tree but hate its fruit, or they love the fruit but hate the tree."

From Jn 8:25, "They said to him, 'Who are you?'" "Jesus said to them, 'Why do I speak to you at all?'"

The reprimand of the third paragraph makes the first paragraph by the disciples into one critical of Jesus. Jesus many have been speaking critically of excessive commitment to the details of the Law of Moses.

The tree in the third paragraph is likely (Jewish) God. The Judeans are (rhetorically) split into those who love God, but hate its fruit who is Jesus;...(now the tree becomes Jesus) or hate the tree (who is Jesus) and love the fruit which is faith, morality, miracles, uplifting preaching.

This type of sophisticated, mystical, turnabout, unintelligible preaching occurs often in both Thomas and the canonical gospels. Again, it serves no purpose of the Gnostics and it is unlikely that its author was anyone but Jesus. It seems to be a criticism of the scribes and Pharisees.

44. Jesus said, "Whoever blasphemes against the Father will be forgiven, and whoever blasphemes against the son will be forgiven, but whoever blasphemes against the Holy Spirit will not be forgiven, either on earth or in heaven."

From Mk 3:28, "Truly I tell you, people will be forgiven for their sins and whatever blasphemies they utter; but whoever blasphemes against the Holy Spirit can never have forgiveness, but is guilty of an eternal sin.", also Mt 12:32, Lk 12:10.

The Holy Spirit is the bringer of all Christ's gifts, including forgiveness. If we repel the Holy Spirit, the graces of forgiveness cannot be given to us. If we blaspheme the Holy Spirit, then repent of it, the Holy Spirit will deliver the forgiveness of Christ to us.

45. Jesus said, "Grapes are not harvested from thorn trees, nor are figs gathered from thistles, for they yield no fruit."

"Good persons produce good from what they've stored up; bad persons produce evil from the wickedness they've stored up in their hearts, and say evil things. For from the overflow of the heart they produce evil."

From Mt 7:16, "You will know them by their fruits. Are grapes gathered from thorns, or figs from thistles? In the same way, every good tree bears good fruit, but the bad tree bears bad fruit. A good tree cannot bear bad fruit, nor can a bad tree bear good fruit. Every tree that does not bear good fruit is cut down and thrown into the fire. Thus you will know them by their fruits."

46. Jesus said, "From Adam to John the Baptist, among those born of women, no one is so much greater than John the Baptist that his eyes should not be averted."

"But I have said that whoever among you becomes a child will recognize the kingdom of God, and will become greater than John."

From Mt 11:11, "Truly I tell you, among those born of women no one has arisen greater than John the Baptist; yet the least in the kingdom of heaven is greater than he."

47. Jesus said, "A person cannot mount two horses or bend two bows."

"And a slave cannot serve two masters, otherwise that slave will honor the one and offend the other."

"Nobody drinks aged wine and immediately wants to drink young wine. Young wine is not poured into old wineskins, or they might break, and aged wine is not poured into a new wineskin, or it might spoil."

"An old patch is not sewn onto a new garment, since it would create a tear."

From Mt 6:24, "No one can serve two masters; for a slave will either hate the one and love the other, or be devoted to the one and despise the other. You cannot serve God and wealth."

From Mt 9:16-17, "No one sews a piece of unshrunk cloth on an old cloak, for the patch pulls away from the cloak, and a worse tear is made. Neither is new wine put into old wineskins; otherwise, the skins burst, and the wine is spilled, and the skins are destroyed; but new wine is put into fresh wineskins, and so both are preserved."

48. Jesus said, "If two make peace with each other in a single house, they will say to the mountain, 'Move from here!' and it will move."

From Mt 18:19, "Again, truly I tell you, if two of you agree on earth about anything you ask, it will be done for you by my Father in heaven."

From Mk 11:23, "Truly I tell you, if you say to this mountain, 'Be taken up and thrown into the sea'...it will be done for them."

Forgiveness is a virtue that can only have its origin in the eternal virtues of God, (specifically Christ). By participating in forgiveness we participate in the virtues, and therefore the person of Christ. As a member of Christ, mountains are at his command.

49. Jesus said, "Congratulations to those who are alone and chosen, for you will find the kingdom. For you have come from it, and you will return there again."

From Lk 14:18-20, "...they all began to make excuses. The first one said, 'I have bought a field and I need to go see it. Please excuse me.' Another said, 'I have bought five yoke of oxen and I am going to try them out. Please excuse' me. Still another said, 'I have married a wife, so I cannot come.'"

Those who have a spouse, children or business are necessarily committed in part to these. Those alone have a head start in complete dedication to God, and union with Christ. Jesus notes that we come from God (Christ) and return to Christ, as a member of the larger body of Christ.

50. Jesus said, "If they say to you, 'Where have you come from?' say to them, 'We have come from the light, from the place where the light came into being by itself, established itself, and appeared in their image.'"

"If they say to you, 'Is it you?' say, 'We are its children, and we are the chosen of the living Father.'"

“If they ask you, 'What is the evidence of your Father in you?' say to them, 'It is motion and rest.'”

Paragraph one in order: We have come from the light of the human race, who is Jesus; we come from Heaven (we now participate in Heaven who is Christ); we come from Christ, the Son of God who came into being by himself and took on a human incarnation, (fully God and fully human).

Paragraph two: “Are you saying you are God?” “We are children of God, and chosen by the Father.”

Paragraph three: “What evidence do you offer?” “The virtue (motion) and peace (rest) of the Father.”

The real possibility exists that the sayings of Thomas were not included into the early canon, because people were still trying to figure them out. We now have 2000 years of study of theology and this gives us an advantage, not fully had in the early church.

51. His disciples said to him, "When will the rest for the dead take place, and when will the new world come?"

“He said to them, "What you are looking forward to has come, but you don't know it."

Rest for the dead is their final peace or fulfillment. It is not so much a time, as the person of Christ, who we join, and it should be occurring now. The new world is not only the place of Heaven, but the person that Heaven is contained within, Jesus. We observe that all creation was contained as ideas within Christ, prior to him giving it creation. Now, the new perfected world (Heaven and the resurrection) is still contained within Jesus, in its divine, uncreated form which we are invited to.

52. His disciples said to him, "Twenty-four prophets have spoken in Israel, and they all spoke of you."

He said to them, "You have disregarded the living one who is in your presence, and have spoken of the dead."

Here Jesus refers to the physically dead, but virtuous prophets. To add to the confusion, Jesus often used the word 'dead' to refer to the spiritually dead or condemned.

53. His disciples said to him, "Is circumcision useful or not?"

He said to them, "If it were useful, their father would produce children already circumcised from their mother. Rather, the true circumcision in spirit has become profitable in every respect."

Related gospel teachings: Rm 2:25-29, 1 Cor 7:17-19, Gal 6:16, Phil 3:3, Col 2:11-14. Recall that in rebuilding humanity after the fall, God chose the tribe of Abraham. The only real requirement was circumcision, (the extensive Law of Moses came later). Circumcision was a sign that God and Abraham were mutually committed to each other; it was belief in God, which is the first act of faith.

Circumcision in spirit is to bond ones spirit to God, as its exclusive God. From this bonding all else may grow if we cultivate it.

54. Jesus said, "Congratulations to the poor, for to you belongs Heaven's kingdom."

Mt 6:20, "Then he looked up at his disciples and said: 'Blessed are you who are poor, for yours is the kingdom of God.'"

The poor who have no excess desire for wealth are at an advantage in that they have fewer burdens of desire, and may direct their entire will toward God. Most importantly is to be 'poor in spirit', or detached from the riches of the world, (Mt 5:3).

55. Jesus said, "Whoever does not hate father and mother cannot be my disciple, and whoever does not

hate brothers and sisters, and carry the cross as I do, will not be worthy of me."

From Mt 10:37, "Whoever loves father or mother more than me is not worthy of me; and whoever loves son or daughter more than me is not worthy of me; and whoever does not take up the cross and follow me is not worthy of me."

Luke 14:26, "If any one comes to me without hating his father and mother, wife and children, brothers and sisters, and even his own life, he cannot be my disciple.

Observe that Mt 10:37 calls us to love Christ more than family, while Lk 14:26 calls us to hate family. Christ spoke both versions, but used the term 'hate' in the meaning of detachment. Just as love is commitment to, hate is detachment from.

Jesus demands that we love all other persons, but be detached from them, so as to be committed to himself. Love which is corrupted into self seeking is lust, and it is this which we must avoid.

One form of self seeking is failure to carry our cross, as Jesus demands of us in this saying. Our salvation is to become the very person of Christ, but we cannot do this if we remain self. The divine doctor himself will see to this soul transplant, our part is to enable it by detachment from self and its more vicious mutation which is sin.

Different wording of the same gospel teachings occurred not only because of human memory, but because Jesus used the same core parables in his daily preaching for three years, and his wording varied more or less.

56. Jesus said, "Whoever has come to know the world has discovered a carcass, and whoever has discovered a carcass, of that person the world is not worthy."

This makes sense if: he who (with moral effort) comes to know the true nature of our fallen world, knows that he has discovered a corpse, or one who is dead (spiritually dead).

This realization, hatred or detachment from the world is the first step toward Christ, who is in this world, but not of it. In a way, Jesus is saying that the world is not worthy of himself.

We observe that many of the simpler sayings of Thomas had their canonical parallels included in the New Testament, while many of the more abstruse sayings of Jesus were perhaps not understood and not included. The book of Revelation was nearly not included into the canon because of its extreme mysticism. We owe a great debt to 2000 years of mystical writings of the saints in interpreting the sayings of Thomas.

57 Jesus said, "The Father's kingdom is like a person who has good seed. His enemy came during the night and sowed weeds among the good seed. The person did not let the workers pull up the weeds, but said to them, 'No, otherwise you might go to pull up the weeds and pull up the wheat along with them.' For on the day of the harvest the weeds will be conspicuous, and will be pulled up and burned."

From Mt 13:24, "He put before them another parable: 'The kingdom of heaven may be compared to someone who sowed good seed in his field; but while everybody was asleep, an enemy came and sowed weeds among the wheat, and then went away. So when the plants came up and bore grain, then the weeds appeared as well. And the slaves of the householder came and said to him, 'Master, did you not sow good seed in your field? Where then, did these weeds come from?' He answered, 'An enemy has done this.' The slaves said to him, 'Then do you want us to go and gather them?' But he replied, 'No; for in gathering the weeds you would uproot the wheat along with them. Let both of them grow together until the harvest; and at harvest time I will tell the reapers, Collect the weeds first and bind them in bundles to be burned, but gather the wheat into my barn.'"

58. Jesus said, "Congratulations to the person who has toiled and has found life."

Our inclusion into the kingdom of God (who is Christ), requires moral effort since we start off with a burden of original sin, which usually snowballs into a greater burden until we come to our senses.

59. Jesus said, "Look to the living one as long as you live, otherwise you might die and then try to see the living one, and you will be unable to see."

From Jn 7:34, "You will search for me, but you will not find me; and where I am, you cannot come."

From Jn 13:33, "Little children, I am with you only a little longer. You will look for me; and as I said to the Jews so now I say to you, 'Where I am going, you cannot come.'"

60. He saw a Samaritan carrying a lamb and going to Judea. He said to his disciples, "Why is that person carrying around the lamb.' They said to him, 'So that he may kill it and eat it.' He said to them, 'He will not eat it while it is alive, but only after he has killed it and it has become a carcass.'"

They said, "Otherwise he can't do it."

He said to them, "So also with you, seek for yourselves a place for rest, or you might become a carcass and be eaten."

Here the third sentence is the teaching: find rest or fulfillment (in Christ), otherwise the devil will devour you. Strictly speaking, all who are not (at some point) members of Jesus Christ (the body of Christ), cannot attain Heaven, who is the person of Christ. Our intended destiny was not to remain in the human perfection of Adam and Eve, but to advance in soul and return as fully mature children of God, (CCC 398).

As designed, our human limitations gave less awareness of the law of God, than the angels had. Our successful lives in these conditions would have been a spiritual advancement, which we would bring with us when we rejoined Christ. Intervening sin (which was never intended) made our conquest of it all the more profitable in our spiritual growth. God cannot grow in love, but he has found a way, by becoming the human and sacrificial Christ, and by inclusion of those who lead a successful life in our fallen world.

From CCC 398, "...man was destined to be fully "divinized" by God in glory...". Redemption of sin was not the original reason for Christ (since sin was never intended), communion was the reason. Sin was an unintended obstacle that Jesus Christ overcame, before he could make his originally intended communion with humanity.

From 2Pet 1:4, "Through these, he has bestowed on us the precious and very great promises, so that through them you may come to share in the divine nature, after escaping from the corruption that is in the world because of evil desire."

From Mt 25:34, "Then the king will say to those on his right, 'Come, you who are blessed by my Father. Inherit the kingdom prepared for you from the foundation of the world.'" As planned, God (Christ) intended us to go into creation and then return to his divine person.

61. Jesus said, "Two will recline on a couch; one will die, one will live."

Salome said, "Who are you mister? You have climbed onto my couch and eaten from my table as if you are from someone."

Jesus said to her, "I am the one who comes from what is whole. I was granted from the things of my Father."

"I am your disciple."

"For this reason I say, if one is whole, one will be filled with light, but if one is divided, one will be filled with darkness."

From Lk 17:34, "I tell you, on that night there will be two in one bed; one will be taken and the other left.". The Whole One Jesus refers to is the Father. The corruption of wholeness is sin (God himself cannot be corrupted), which is lacking in its original wholeness. Self seeking usurps that portion of virtue which should be directed to God or others; corrupted moderation becomes greed or hoarding, respect becomes arrogance. Sin is a lacking, but since our virtues are active, our corrupted or lacking virtues are also active, and sin takes on a proactive nature of evil.

62. Jesus said, "I disclose my mysteries to those [who are worthy] of [my] mysteries."

"Do not let your left hand know what your right hand is doing."

Words in brackets [...] are damaged portions of the manuscript. Here we again observe the pattern of selflessness (and the sacraments) leading to inclusion into the body of Christ, after which we share in the larger world of Christ.

Even before the advent of the body of Christ, with Jesus, God revealed eternal spiritual truths to those seeking them, and even beyond Judaism, all were his children and God saw to their spiritual well being primarily, but not exclusively by their moral conscience.

The second paragraph is a shorter version of Mt 6:3, "But when you give alms, do not let your left hand know what your right hand is doing.". It encourages giving alms in secret, to the extent that the idle hand does not know what the giving hand is doing.

63 Jesus said, "There was a rich person who had a great deal of money. He said, 'I shall invest my money so that I may sow, reap, plant, and fill my storehouses with produce, that I may lack nothing.' These were the things he was thinking in his heart, but that very night he died. Anyone here with two ears had better listen!"

Lk 12:16-20, "Then he told them a parable: 'The land of a rich man produced abundantly. And he thought to himself, 'What should I do, for I have no place to store my crops?' Then he said, 'I will do this: I will pull down my barns and build larger ones, and there I will store all my grain and my goods. And I will say to my soul, 'Soul, you have ample goods laid up for many years; relax, eat, drink, be merry.' But God said to him, 'You fool! This very night your life is being demanded of you.'"

64. Jesus said, "A person was receiving guests. When he had prepared the dinner, he sent his slave to invite the guests."

"The slave went to the first and said to that one, 'My master invites you.' That one said, 'Some merchants owe me money; they are coming to me tonight. I have to go and give them instructions. Please excuse me from dinner.'"

"The slave went to another and said to that one, 'My master has invited you.' That one said to the slave, 'I have bought a house, and I have been called away for a day. I shall have no time.'"

"The slave went to another and said to that one, 'My master invites you.' That one said to the slave, 'My friend is to be married, and I am to arrange the banquet. I shall not be able to come. Please excuse me from dinner.'"

"The slave went to another and said to that one, 'My master invites you.' That one said to the slave, 'I have

bought an estate, and I am going to collect the rent. I shall not be able to come. Please excuse me.'"

"The slave returned and said to his master, 'Those whom you invited to dinner have asked to be excused.' The master said to his slave, 'Go out on the streets and bring back whomever you find to have dinner.'"

"Buyers and merchants [will] not enter the places of my Father."

From Lk 14:16, "Then Jesus said to him, 'A man gave agave a great dinner and invited many. At the time for the dinner he sent his slave to say to those who had been invited, 'Come; for everything is ready now.' But they all alike began to make excuses. The first said to him, 'I have bought a piece of land, and I must go out and see it; please accept my regrets.' Another said, 'I have bought five yoke of oxen, and I am going to try them out; please accept my regrets.' Another said, 'I have just been married, and therefore I cannot come.' So the slave returned and reported this to his master. Then the owner of the house became angry and said to his slave, 'Go out at once into the streets and lanes of the town and bring in the poor, the crippled, the blind, and the lame.' And the slave said, 'Sir, what you ordered has been done, and there is still room." Then the master said to the slave, 'Go out into the roads and lanes, and compel people to come in, so that my house may be filled. For I tell you, none of those who were invited will taste my dinner.'"

In both the canonical and Gospel of Thomas, Jesus speaks in hyperbole, or exaggeration. Virtually no one could be saved if God were only strict justice. Look at the last paragraph in Thomas, "Buyers and merchants will not enter the places of my Father.". This sound bite in isolation would be considered at variance with Catholic teaching. The sayings of the Gospel of Thomas are far more isolated than the canonical gospels, and we must acknowledge this as we study it. We could even isolate the canonical gospels to the point of error, and it has been done.

65. He said, "A [...] person owned a vineyard and rented it to some farmers, so they could work it and he could collect its crop from them. He sent his slave so the farmers would give him the vineyard's crop. They grabbed him, beat him, and almost killed him, and the slave returned and told his master. His master said, 'Perhaps he didn't know them.' He sent another slave, and the farmers beat that one as well. Then the master sent his son and said, 'Perhaps they'll show my son some respect.' Because the farmers knew that he was the heir to the vineyard, they grabbed him and killed him. Anyone here with two ears had better listen!"

In the first sentence the brackets [...], is a damaged portion of papyrus in the manuscript, here the word "wealthy" would be a predictable fit. Some scholars can discern the word "good", where Christ would be the good man who rented out his vineyard. The saying is of course the gospel parable of the tenants, Mt 21:33-43.

66. Jesus said, "Show me the stone that the builders rejected: that is the keystone."

From Lk 20:17, "But he looked at them and said, 'What then does this text mean: the stone that the builders rejected has become the cornerstone?'". In building we have the sense not to reject a good stone, but due to spiritual myopia the priests and Pharisees, (and ourselves) too often reject Christ, in part or full, but Christ is the foundation upon which all else is built.

67 Jesus said, "Whoever believes that the All is lacking is himself completely lacking."

God is the All, and if we believe that God is anything less than eternal, absolute, and complete; then we are lacking in knowledge of God. Again, why would anyone else forge this, it supports only monotheism. Gnosticism is full of semi-gods and sinful gods.

None of the sayings that appear only in the Gospel of Thomas, specifically support Gnosticism. If one were to study the beliefs of (the many variations) of Gnosticism. He could easily rewrite the teachings of Jesus to support, or at least mention their ideas of the demiurge (the corrupt god who created our world), or the semi-divine Aeons, or the three groups of people: the unconditionally saved, the conditionally saved, the unconditionally condemned.

68 Jesus said, "Blessed are you when you are hated and persecuted; and no place will be found, wherever you have been persecuted."

From Mt 5:11, "Blessed are you when people revile you and persecute you and utter all kinds of evil against you falsely on my account."

From Mt 10:23, "When you are persecuted in one place, flee to another..."

69 Jesus said, "Blessed are those who have been persecuted in their hearts: they are the ones who have truly come to know the Father."

"Blessed are those who go hungry, for the belly of him who desires will be filled."

To be 'persecuted in heart' is to undergo moral trial of the will. This trial is God reaching out to us, to make us realize our imperfect actions. This minimal realization alone is a sort of repentance. We are then called to correct or thoughts, will and actions.

The second part is similar to "Blessed are the poor". It could also refer to fasting, which denies even a legitimate self need. This detachment from self facilitates a deepened participation in Christ. Fasting is considered a useful spiritual tool in the Catholic Church.

70. Jesus said, "If you bring forth what is within you, what you have will save you. If you do not have that within you, what you do not have within you will kill you."

If we allow Jesus his poetic preaching, and add some theology, Christ's initial omnipresence in us can be brought forth or cultivated into sanctifying grace and we are saved. If we fail to do this we risk spiritual death (Hell) by God's judgment.

Christ's omnipresence is Christ sustaining us in being. It is a non-moral quality given to everything, if it ceased, we would cease to exist. In this saying, Christ cultivates us from an intelligent but self-obedient entity to a mature and real child of God. Christ is at least minimally in everything by the non-moral virtue of being. Sanctifying grace (Catholic speak for salvation), adds this final layer of grace to our initial grace of being.

71. Jesus said, "I will destroy [this] house, and no one will be able to build it [...]."

'This house', which Jesus will destroy cannot be Jesus himself, it must be the temple, (Mt 22:4). It is a sound bite which must have had significant ideas leading to it. The words in brackets are damaged in the manuscript. The empty brackets are words of the manuscript that are missing due to damage and decomposition.

72. A [person said] to him, "Tell my brothers to divide my father's possessions with me."

He said to the person, "Mister, who made me a divider?"

He turned to his disciples and said to them, "I'm not a divider, am I?"

From Lk 12:13, "Someone in the crowd said to him, 'Teacher, tell my brother to divide the family inheritance with me.' But he said to him, 'Friend, who set me to be a judge or arbitrator over you?'"

In both Thomas and the canonical gospels Jesus claims to be both a divider (Lk 12:51), and not to be a divider, (Lk 12:13). In Lk 12:51 he foreshadows our final judgement; in Lk 12:13, he encourages sharing and detachment of wealth.

73. Jesus said, "The crop is huge but the workers are few, so beg the harvest boss to dispatch workers to the fields."

This is a virtual retelling of Mt 9:37-38. The workers dispatched for the harvest or bringing in of souls are Christians who are literally Christ in our world. They continue his redemptive mission by giving the sacraments, and most vitally by the remediation of sin into virtue, allowing the incorporation of the individual into the perfect person of Christ.

74. He said, "Lord, there are many around the drinking trough, but there is nothing in the well."

This is clearly not spoken by Jesus, but to Jesus. It could mean many things. Perhaps there is a dry well which Jesus miraculously fills. Jesus also repeatedly taught that the Law of Moses itself could not save; perhaps a Pharisee comes to this knowledge and states this in figurative speech.

75. Jesus said, "There are many standing at the door, but those who are alone will enter the bridal suite."

This is related to Luke 14:26, "If any one comes to me without hating his father and mother, wife and children...". Those who are alone may devote their will entirely to Christ, when their will is fulfilled, they become members of Christ, who is now the entire body of Christ.

In fact we must love all others, that means that we are committed in will to them. Literal aloneness is not demanded once we go beyond this isolated verse.

In the beatitudes (Matthew 5:1-12), Jesus does not demand actual poverty, but 'poverty in spirit', this is a matter of not desiring wealth, rather than not having wealth.

76. Jesus said, "The Father's kingdom is like a merchant who had a supply of merchandise and found a pearl. That merchant was prudent; he sold the merchandise and bought the single pearl for himself."

"So also with you, seek his treasure that is unfailing, that is enduring, where no moth comes to eat and no worm destroys."

From Mt 13:45-46, "Again, the kingdom of heaven is like a merchant in search of fine pearls; on finding one pearl of great value, he went and sold all that he had and bought it."

The wise person will detach from all other persons and things and pursue only the kingdom of Heaven.

77. Jesus said, "I am the light that is over all things. I am all: from me all came forth, and to me all attained."

"Split a piece of wood; I am there."

"Lift up the stone, and you will find me there."

The first paragraph combines the gospel ideas of Jn 1:3 (all things came into being through Jesus), and Rev 22:13, ("I am the Alpha and the Omega, the first and the last, the beginning and the end.").

The second and third paragraphs are not pantheism (God is all things), but divine omnipresence (God is in all things). At a minimum Christ's attribute of being exists in all things. If something did not have the attribute of being, it would not exist, or cease to exist. This attribute of being may be given by extended means, but it must have its origin and its own ongoing existence in God. If God ceased to think of something or ceased to will it, it would cease to be. God not only knows everything (divine omniscience), but God has a presence in everything, and sustains everything, which we call divine omnipresence.

This idea was written of by Doctor of the Church, St. Thomas Aquinas, (Summa Theologica, first part, question 8, article 1); he went so far as to say God has a non-moral presence even in demons, (they were created as angels with the attribute of being, and as devils they retain this non-moral attribute of being), if not they would cease to exist. From this we can easily see that creator Christ is present in the wood and the stone mentioned in the Gospel of Thomas.

The doctrine appears in the 1912 Catholic Encyclopedia, which is free, online, and gives a good explanation under the heading "God, attributes of":

> *"...God is really present everywhere in creation, not merely in virtue of operation, but in virtue of essence. In other words God Himself, or the Divine nature, is in immediate contact with, or immanent in, every creature — conserving it in being and enabling it to act."*

78. Jesus said, "Why have you come out to the countryside? To see a reed shaken by the wind? And to see a person dressed in soft clothes, [like your] rulers and your powerful ones? They are dressed in soft clothes, and they cannot understand truth."

Mt 11:7-9, "As they went away, Jesus began to speak to the crowds about John: 'What did you go out into the wilderness to look at? A reed shaken by the wind? What then did you go out to see? Someone dressed in soft robes? Look, those who wear soft robes are in royal palaces. What then did you go out to see? A prophet? Yes, I tell you, and more than a prophet.'"

Jesus is speaking about John the Baptist. As to the last sentence, it is the established teaching that indulgence of self, prohibits by degree a deeper sharing outside of self, in the person of Christ.

79. A woman in the crowd said to him, "Lucky is the womb that bore you and the breasts that fed you."

"He said to [her], "Lucky are those who have heard the word of the Father and have truly kept it. For there will be days when you will say, 'Lucky are the womb that has not conceived and the breasts that have not given milk.'"

From Lk 11:27-28, "While he was saying this, a woman in the crowd raised her voice and said to him, 'Blessed is the womb that bore you and the breasts that nursed you!' But he said, 'Blessed rather are those who hear the word of God and obey it!'

80. Jesus said, "Whoever has come to know the world has discovered the body, and whoever has discovered the body, of that one the world is not worthy."

Virtually identical to Gospel of Thomas saying 56, see comments there.

81. Jesus said, "Let one who has become wealthy reign, and let one who has power renounce it."

At first glance the two phrases seem to contradict, since they give positive and negative views on wealth and power, which in the days of Jesus were synonymous.

If we make 'one who has wealth', into 'one who is rich in the things of God', then he should reign, while the one who has worldly power should give it up to seek Christ, who cannot dwell in those full of self and self interest.

82. Jesus said, "Whoever is near me is near the fire, and whoever is far from me is far from the (Father's) kingdom."

Jesus refers to himself as the fire. A fire gives off light, Jesus is the light of God. The second part of the teaching has those who are far from Jesus as far from the kingdom of God.

This saying in the Gospel of Thomas is quoted by Pope Benedict XVI in his Easter vigil Mass on Holy Saturday, 7 April 2012. The early Church theologian Origen also reports this saying to have been spoken by Jesus.

83. Jesus said, "Images are visible to people, but the light within them is hidden in the image of the Father's light. He will be disclosed, but his image is hidden by his light."

(The light of) Christ is the image of the Father, (Jn 14:9, "Anyone who has seen me has seen the Father."). The Father will be disclosed in spirit, (we will finally see God, Mt 5:8), but until we are able to bear it, he remains as human Jesus Christ.

The same explanation side by side: "Images are visible to people", (drop this phrase and proceed); "The light within them (Jesus Christ), is in the image of the Father", (Jesus is the image of the Father). "He will be disclosed" (in Heaven), "But (for now) his image is hidden by his light", (his light or image is Jesus).

84. Jesus said, "When you see your likeness, you are happy. But when you see your images that came into being before you and that neither die nor become visible, how much you will have to bear!"

We are an eternal idea within God. When we are given creation, the (perfect) idea of us within God does not cease. Perhaps (in Heaven) we will be given knowledge of God's perfect idea of us, it could be a lot to bear. This ideal would be compared to our actual spiritual attainment.

The Marian apparition of Garabandal alludes to a worldwide revelation of conscious, which may be similar.

Perhaps Jesus is referring to such a personal revelation at the death of each of us.

85. Jesus said, "Adam came from great power and great wealth, but he was not worthy of you. For had he been worthy, [he would] not [have tasted] death."

This is Jesus speaking to disciple Christians who are saved, and share in the body of Christ. Strictly speaking this participation in the body of Christ, first occurred at the Eucharist of the last supper, but Jesus does not discourage the good news with details of sequence. At times Jesus disregarded salvation sequence in the canonical gospels.

Adam, even in his pre-sinful state did not enjoy stature as a member of Christ (the body of Christ), and is lesser than a member of Christ. This is similar to the teaching in Mt 11:11, that the least in the divine kingdom of Heaven is greater than the great human prophet John the Baptist.

Again the Catholic teaching on membership in the body of Christ is that we first share in the human nature of Jesus Christ, (which explains why we do walk around divine); then in Heaven we share in the full divine nature of Christ, (CCC 398). It is possible to share in the divine nature of Christ on earth, the mystical marriage of the saints occurs between them and divine Christ, once they have perfected their will on earth. Since divinization was our intended destiny (CCC 398), and sin was never part of God's plan for humanity, our divine participation was to have occurred in this life. It still may for those willing to put in the moral effort.

The book "Mystical Evolution" by Fr. John Arintero is a detailed examination of our spiritual evolution from humanity to divinization. It makes extensive examination of the divine marriage or union of the saints; this is the Heavenly wedding that Jesus speaks of. It is the actual divine communion between God and man.

86. Jesus said, "[Foxes have their dens] and birds have [their] nests, but the son of man has no place to lay his head and rest."

From Mt 8:20, "And Jesus said to him, "Foxes have holes, and birds of the air have nests; but the Son of Man has nowhere to lay his head."

87. Jesus said, "How miserable is the body that depends on a body, and how miserable is the soul that depends on these two."

Our body who depends only upon itself (and has not dependence or sharing in God) is miserable. Our soul (will, intellect, memory, virtues, emotions, all our spiritual attributes) that does not venture further than itself, into God is even that much more miserable.

88. Jesus said, "The messengers and the prophets will come to you and give you what belongs to you. You, in turn, give them what you have, and say to yourselves, 'When will they come and take what belongs to them?'"

The prophets and missionaries will offer to you, your inheritance which is a sharing in the life and person of Christ, who is God. We then offer (to God, via the sacraments) all that we have, both virtue and sin; thought and will, body and soul. Then we await eagerly our Heavenly communion to Christ.

It is within the bounds of Catholic teaching that God uses Heavenly angels, dominions and powers to operate both Heaven and earth. The book of Revelation has angels making all sorts of errands between Heaven and earth, as do other books of the bible. It is not impossible for instance that the angels escort Christ to the Eucharist, and take our prayers to Heaven. St. Suso saw the angel assigned to oversee the virtue of speech, he was one of the rebellious angels and was now assigned by the devil to oversee blasphemy. It is also possible that this saying is partially figurative, setting up an ideal world of interaction.

89. Jesus said, "Why do you wash the outside of the cup? Don't you understand that the one who made the inside is also the one who made the outside?"

A scenario that works is that the outside of the cup is our body and we are concerned for it, but God also made our soul which we should also be concerned for. This teaching may have been made to the general public, who would have been driven by worry of food and clothing. The Pharisees also, were concerned with ritual purity and avoided contamination, and this could have limited their spiritual growth.

90. Jesus said, "Come to me, for my yoke is comfortable and my lordship is gentle, and you will find rest for yourselves."

This is a near identical retelling of Mt 11:28-30. Christ does not demand success in business, health, wealth, or ritual piety. In fact the more unencumbered our lives are, the faster we may deepen our sharing in the virtues and life of Christ, which is the only thing Jesus demands of us.

91. They said to him, "Tell us who you are so that we may believe in you."

He said to them, "You examine the face of heaven and earth, but you have not come to know the one who is in your presence, and you do not know how to examine the present moment."

Many disciples were slow to acknowledge Jesus as the Christ Messiah. In fairness the first paragraph shows prudent caution, as in Israel there was always someone claiming to be Messiah.

Lk 12:56, "...why do you not know how to interpret the present time?". The present time was a time of special grace, with Jesus in the world for only a few years. Now was the time for Israel to make its prophesied fulfillment in the Messiah.

92. Jesus said, "Seek and you will find."

"In the past, however, I did not tell you the things about which you asked me then. Now I am willing to tell them, but you are not seeking them."

Mt 7:7, "Ask, and it will be given you; search, and you will find; knock, and the door will be opened for you."

From the second paragraph we learn that Jesus did not reveal all the mysteries of God, salvation and the future at once. His prophecy of the destruction of the temple, the tribulation and his own death all came later. His theology of the Eucharist was revealed half way through his ministry, and many left him.

93. "Don't give what is holy to dogs, for they might throw them upon the manure pile. Don't throw pearls [to] pigs, or they might ... it [...]."

Mt 7:6, "Do not give what is holy to dogs; and do not throw your pearls before swine, or they will trample them under foot and turn and maul you."

94. Jesus [said], "One who seeks will find, and for [one who knocks] it will be opened."

Mt 7:8, "For everyone who asks receives, and everyone who searches finds, and for everyone who knocks, the door will be opened."

95. [Jesus said], "If you have money, don't lend it at interest. Rather, give [it] to someone from whom you won't get it back."

Lk 6:34-35, "If you lend to those from whom you hope to receive, what credit is that to you? Even sinners lend to sinners, to receive as much again. But love your enemies, do good and lend, expecting nothing in return."

96. Jesus [said], "The Father's kingdom is like [a] woman. She took a little leaven, [hid] it in dough, and made it into large loaves of bread. Anyone here with two ears had better listen!"

Mt 13:33, "He told them another parable: "The kingdom of heaven is like yeast that a woman took and mixed in with three measures of flour until all of it was leavened." This verse seems to be positive, but Jesus also warned the disciples against, "The yeast of the Pharisees.".

97. Jesus said, "The [Father's] kingdom is like a woman who was carrying a [jar] full of meal. While she was walking along [a] distant road, the handle of the jar broke and the meal spilled behind her [along] the road. She didn't know it; she hadn't noticed a problem. When she reached her house, she put the jar down and discovered that it was empty."

This is a warning parable, similar to Lk 19:26, "He replied, 'I tell you that to everyone who has, more will be given, but as for the one who has nothing, even what they have will be taken away." It is similar also to Gospel of Thomas saying 41.

The theology is as follows: What we call judgment is actually God's originally intended communion with a person, (see notes following saying 60). Christ makes the communion, rejoining all goodness to himself, all evil and those owning it will be unable to make the communion, the evil left behind is Hell. From this saying and the gospel verses we see that it is possible that "even what we think we have, will be taken from us." See also the appendix for an explanation of the process of Hell.

98. Jesus said, "The Father's kingdom is like a person who wanted to kill someone powerful. While still at home he drew his sword and thrust it into the wall to find out whether his hand would go in. Then he killed the powerful one."

This is somewhat similar to Lk 14:31, "Or what king, when he sets out to meet another king in battle, will not first sit down and consider whether he is strong enough with ten thousand men to encounter the one coming against him with twenty thousand?". In this saying the powerful man to be killed is likely the devil. The assailant (who is the Christian), trains to defeat the devil, then does so.

99. The disciples said to him, "Your brothers and your mother are standing outside."

"He said to them, 'Those here who do what my Father wants are my brothers and my mother. They are the ones who will enter my Father's kingdom.'"

This is a virtual retelling of Mt 12:46-50, "While he was still speaking to the crowds, his mother and his brothers were standing outside, wanting to speak to him. Someone told him, 'Look, your mother and your brothers are standing outside, wanting to speak to you.' But to the one who had told him this, Jesus replied, 'Who is my mother, and who are my brothers?' And pointing to his disciples, he said, 'Here are my mother and my brothers! For whoever does the will of my Father in heaven is my brother and sister and mother.'"

We might rephrase the last sentence, "Whoever does the will of the Father, is now rejoined to me as the body of Christ." In the body of Christ we will not lose our attributes of: brother sister, mother. Since we will all share in one another (Rm 12:5), the mother of one member is the mother of all members, including Jesus who is the preeminent member of the body of Christ.

100. They showed Jesus a gold coin and said to him, "The Roman emperor's people demand taxes from us."

"He said to them, 'Give the emperor what belongs to the emperor, give God what belongs to God, and give me what is mine.'"

This is the famous wit of Jesus in Mk 12:14-17.

101. "Whoever does not hate [father] and mother as I do cannot be my [disciple], and whoever does [not] love [father and] mother as I do cannot be my [disciple]. For my mother [...], but my true [mother] gave me life."

This is a variation of saying 55, which is similar to Mt 10:37 and Lk 14:26. This saying demands proper love and hate (commitment to and detachment from) father and mother. As to the last sentence, the idea is that every (good) attribute in our world, including fatherhood and motherhood necessarily has its origin in the person of God, (and specifically Christ, who brought forth all of creation). If God is the father of Jesus, he is necessarily also the mother of Jesus.

The single blank bracket [...], might be filled in with "gave me humanity". We observe that the mother of Jesus is the Blessed Virgin Mary, who noble as she is, is a conduit of God's graces, not their origin. Jesus had 'true life', from the beginning of course, but this is a teaching to others on our greater life beyond this one.

102. Jesus said, "Woe to the Pharisees! They are like a dog sleeping in the cattle manger: the dog neither eats nor lets the cattle eat."

Similar to Mt 23:13, "Woe to you, teachers of the law and Pharisees, you hypocrites! You shut the door of the kingdom of heaven in people's faces. You yourselves do not enter, nor will you let those enter who are trying to."

The Pharisees were self indulgent in prideful perfection of piety, and criticism of others. They did not enter the kingdom of Heaven, and they said that those less perfect in ritual piety would not enter Heaven. We observe that Purgatory is a possibility for those not entering the kingdom of Heaven.

103. Jesus said, "Congratulations to those who know where the rebels are going to attack. [They] can get going, collect their imperial resources, and be prepared before the rebels arrive."

When we know our failings, we may be on guard to make our better behavior, and ask for assistance from the army of Heaven. Similar to Mt 24:43.

104. They said to Jesus, "Come, let us pray today, and let us fast."

Jesus said, "What sin have I committed, or how have I been undone? Rather, when the groom leaves the bridal suite, then let people fast and pray."

Similar to Mk 2:19, "Jesus answered, 'How can the guests of the bridegroom fast while he is with them? They cannot, so long as they have him with them.'"

105. Jesus said, "Whoever knows the father and the mother will be called the child of a prostitute."

This is strong language from Jesus, It is similar to Mt 10:37 and Lk 14:26, (hate your father, mother, and even your own life). Humanity, sold themselves (like a prostitute) for some corrupt gain, and are now corrupted. This is the story of Adam and Eve, and we are to detach ourselves from our lesser parents and seek our true parent who is God. We observe that God used such harsh language when he called ancient Israel an adulteress, because she was committed to false gods.

106. Jesus said, "When you make the two into one, you will become children of Adam, and when you say, 'Mountain, move from here!' it will move."

We make the two into one, when a person makes union with Jesus Christ. Here Adam enjoys his better status as a child of God. Mk 11:23 tells us to move mountains into the sea by our faith and sharing in Christ.

107. Jesus said, "The Father's kingdom is like a shepherd who had a hundred sheep. One of them, the largest, went astray. He left the ninety-nine and looked for the one until he found it. After he had toiled, he said to the sheep, 'I love you more than the ninety-nine.'"

This is a retelling of Mt 18:12-13, "What do you think? If a shepherd has a hundred sheep, and one of them has gone astray, does he not leave the ninety-nine on the mountains and go in search of the one that went astray? And if he finds it, truly I tell you, he rejoices over it more than over the ninety-nine that never went astray."

One theory as to why Christ loves the strayed sheep (the strayed, sinful person) more, is that he has been given a greater moral burden. In finding the strayed sheep, it means that the sinner has repented and come to God. This sinner perhaps shows a greater love of God, (commitment to God), because of the greater moral effort.

108. Jesus said, "Whoever drinks from my mouth will become like me; I myself shall become that person, and the hidden things will be revealed to him."

To drink from the mouth of Jesus, is to take in his words and teachings. In doing this, we join the body of Christ, who is Jesus himself (and all other members). We will have the knowledge of Christ because we are the person of Christ.

109. Jesus said, "The Father's kingdom is like a person who had a treasure hidden in his field but did not know it. And [when] he died he left it to his [son]. The son [did] not know about it either. He took over the field and sold it. The buyer went plowing, [discovered] the treasure, and began to lend money at interest to whomever he wished."

Here the son is not Jesus, because the son was unaware of the treasure in the field. The final buyer who discovered the treasure (the kingdom of God), shared it with others, and got interest or a reward. The series of unaware field owners could be the people of Israel, prior to the Messiah.

110. Jesus said, "Let one who has found the world, and has become wealthy, renounce the world."

The one who finds the world and discovers its limitations, but chooses instead to become wealthy in the kingdom of God (he in effect renounces the world), is the person Jesus refers to. In the canonical gospels and the Gospel of Thomas, Jesus has a relatively low opinion of this fallen world, because he knows the glory of the kingdom of God.

111. Jesus said, "The heavens and the earth will roll up in your presence, and whoever is living from the living one will not see death."

Does not Jesus say, "Those who have found themselves, of them the world is not worthy"?

Is 66:22 and 2Pet 3:13 both speak of a new Heaven and a new earth. Here Jesus refers to Heaven as being created by

God (angles, thrones, dominions). All of Heaven and earth are intended to have final fulfillment as part of divine Christ, God will be "all in all things", (1Cor 15:28). In this saying, we are not the cause of this, but observers of it.

The second paragraph is a retelling of saying 56. Jesus may have made this teaching repeatedly in his mission.

112. Jesus said, "Curse the flesh that depends on the soul. Curse the soul that depends on the flesh."

Our bodies have been given over to the corruption of sin, we all have physical death. The 'flesh' in the saying is under a certain curse of death. In the second sentence, the soul that does not participate beyond the flesh (into Christ) is also under a curse of spiritual death.

113. His disciples said to him, "When will the kingdom come?"

"It will not come by watching for it. It will not be said, 'Look, here!' or 'Look, there!' Rather, the Father's kingdom is spread out upon the earth, and people don't see it."

Similar to saying three. Jesus tells the disciples that the prophesied kingdom of God will not be a new government or temple, it is here already, and it is he.

114. Simon Peter said to them, "Make Mary leave us, for females don't deserve life."

Jesus said, "Look, I will guide her to make her male, so that she too may become a living spirit resembling you males. For every female who makes herself male will enter the kingdom of Heaven."

The first paragraph is <u>not</u> a teaching of Jesus, it is an emotional explosion of Peter. The author acknowledges Peter as the best of men, but Peter did make moral mistakes:

he abandoned Jesus, and he lied in saying he did not even know Jesus. This saying is another mistaken act of Peter. It is embarrassing, but likely true.

By true or false legend, Mary Magdalene was a notorious prostitute possessed by seven devils, (and just the kind of person Jesus loved). Perhaps Mary applies as a disciple and Peter loudly objects.

We observe that the apostle Thomas of the canonical gospels denied that Jesus had risen after three days, (just as he had promised). Not all the words or actions (even of the apostles) recorded in the canonical gospels are correct or moral. The actions of Judas are recorded, but not all of his actions were good or moral. If Peter's denial of Jesus had not appeared in the canonical gospel, but only in the Gospel of Thomas, we would declare it inauthentic, even though it did in fact happen.

In this Gospel of Thomas saying, Peter is likely speaking of Mary Magdalene. Jesus soundly corrects Peter, "LOOK! I will guide her to make her male…". We are to share in the very person of the <u>man</u> Jesus. The larger truth of the body of Christ is that, "There is neither Jew nor Gentile, neither slave nor free, <u>nor is there male and female</u>, for you are all one in Christ Jesus.", (Gal 3:28).

The body of Christ is now all who share in the life and person of the Son of God: Jesus, angels, Eucharist, humans. They all make up the single person of Christ. In this Thomas saying, Jesus grants Peter his gender idea but says (via Paul) that "We, who are many, are one body in Christ, and individually member's one of another." (Rm 12:5).

______________ooOoo______________

<u>Appendix: Trinity, Jesus Christ, Body of Christ, Hell</u>

(This appendix is relevant articles from the author's book, "A Maximum Understanding of the Body of Christ")

<u>God the Trinity</u>

We cannot speak of God creating any part of himself, but God does progressively reveal himself, to humanity and even to his own self. The Trinity is three divine persons, Father, Son, and Holy Spirit. Not three Gods, but three divine persons, the three of which constitute the one God. The Trinity of God is a mystery—not fully understood, and incapable of full understanding by any human.

Godhead is undifferentiated, unexpressed, absolute and singular being. Godhead is the simple, essential, unified, core God. Godhead is the necessarily first and fundamental revelation of God. Every movement of God — every act of thought, will and love further reveals and defines God. "When" Godhead acts in such a way as to reveal the divine Son, Godhead reveals himself to be God the Father. God makes revelation simply by thinking or willing. When God thinks of himself, his image the Son of God is revealed.[4]

The Trinity is eternal, but far from static. In the Nicene creed, we read (and pray at Mass), that *Christ was <u>begotten</u> of the Father, and the Holy Spirit <u>proceeds</u> from the Father and the Son.* "Before" God was revealed as the Trinity, God was revealed as undifferentiated Godhead.

---

[4] It is interesting to note that God's revelation of specific attributes, and even specific, divine persons (Father, Son, Holy Spirit), from more <u>general</u> attributes has a parallel in cosmology. Science understands the big bang to be a process of a single super dimension, becoming specific dimensions in the first few seconds of time. Time itself devolved from the greater dimension of eternity, which is the unified existence of cause and effect. Thus, eternal being is not outside the limitations of physics.

The revelation of Godhead as the three distinct persons of the Trinity is thought to be non-optional. "When" Godhead thinks, he "first" thinks of himself, (what else, no creation yet). In doing so, Godhead reveals the trait of intellect, beyond the trait of pure being of the Godhead.

When Godhead thinks of himself, he generates the complete image of himself who is the Son of God; and Godhead is now God the Father. The Son of God is the fullest expression of God. The Son of God himself is not yet *fully* revealed; the human children of God are called to be yet more expression of the Son of God, as the body of Christ.

The first and non-optional act of the newly revealed God the Father and God the Son is to love each other.[5] The Father and the Son directing their wills toward each other generates the Holy Spirit. The Holy Spirit may be thought of as the bond of love (commitment) between the Father and the Son.

In example, think of two people having a common pursuit; this might be marriage or a business perhaps. As this pursuit is cultivated it becomes a real separate entity, this third entity becomes more than words. A marriage or a corporation is given a certain legal status and rights of its own. The efforts of the two people give real form to the third entity.

This example is necessarily inadequate. When God thinks and wills however; it is as real as it gets. The love of the Father and the Son toward each other is divine, selfless, full, intense, real, and permanent. Included in these thoughts is the possibility of creation outside of God. The Holy Spirit who results is divine, independent, full, intense and permanent.

---

[5] Love cannot be fully defined, it would be a matter of the part (humanity) trying to observe the whole (God). Love is as elemental as God in the configuration of the Godhead. The Godhead loving itself (no creation or even Trinity yet), may even be free of the emotional elements of love, it is a love which is not dependent upon emotional satisfaction. When the persons of the Trinity are revealed, the personhood of God is revealed; along with its accompanying virtues and emotions of love.

Too often, human love grasps onto the satisfying emotions of love, to the exclusion of virtuous love. We accept love of virtue, so long as we are also emotionally satisfied. In our spiritual development we should reflect always on the elemental love of the Godhead and of the Trinity.

The Holy Spirit is the acting agent of creation, sent by the Father and the Son, and is a real and complete divine person. The Holy Spirit is the result of the mutual willing of the Father and the Son. The Holy Spirit is not necessarily God's *proportional* will. It is possible, even likely that the Holy Spirit is God's compete, but weighted will, with favoritism toward mercy, joy and peace.

Jesus Christ

Jesus is the created human nature of the Trinitarian Son of God. Jesus is the Son of God extended into creation. The doctrine concerning the divine and human natures of Jesus is summarized in the Catechism, CCC 464-483. Existing dogma of this hypostatic (underlying) union limits itself to declaring that in the single divine person of Jesus Christ there existed a complete man, and complete God. Jesus had a human body, soul, intellect and will; and every faculty of God was part of Jesus, including the divine intellect and will. These existed in the one divine person of Jesus Christ; distinctly and functionally, without confusion or opposition.[6]

The *distinct* faculties of soul of Jesus and the Son of God — will, awareness, intellect — are shown by the many instances of Jesus exhibiting will, knowledge and consciousness distinct from God, (Mt.26:39, Jn.6:38, Jn.5:30, Mt.24:36).[7]

---

[6] The early Christian Council of Chalcedon (AD451), declared that the two natures Jesus Christ — the human nature of Jesus, and the divine nature of the Son of God — each retains its own properties and are united in one person of Christ. "Christ" is a title, which has become a name for the entire body of Christ, which now consists of Jesus and many others.

[7] Definitions must be understood when speaking of the person of Christ:

— "Person" is the title given to a moral being. A person is considered human or divine according to his highest mode of existence. Jesus was a complete human man, and completely God. Since Jesus' highest mode of existence is divine, he is considered a divine person.

— "The Son of God" is the second person of the Trinity of God, also called the Trinitarian Christ. The Son of God may include others into his person, and does just this in enlarging the body of Christ. Jesus was not included into the Son of God, but originated from the Son of God.

— "Christ" is all who share in the life of the Son of God. Firstly, the Son of God, then angels, human Jesus and the faithful. Christ is a royal title for all children of God starting with his own Son, and ultimately including all things: Eucharist, the lion who lies down with the lamb, all else. Christ is the

We have likely never considered the idea of one man having two intellects and two wills, (human and divine no less!) which operate seamlessly. There is no dogma as to this operation, but we may feel out an explanation.

We routinely think multiple thoughts. We might be cooking, ironing or even driving while our thoughts are fixed on our family, job or monthly budget. Likewise for our will; we routinely exert our will in two areas simultaneously. We may now envision two minds and two wills working seamlessly within the single person of Christ who had both human and divine natures.

One way to envision this arrangement is to recall the Trinitarian Son of God (who we call Christ), as having a will that was absolute in its principles. The Son of God then extends himself into creation as the human Jesus. Along with the human body, is given a human mind and will. *The human will of Jesus was a subset of the divine will.* Jesus was free to use his human free will within the bounds of the perfect divine will of the Son of God.

The human free will of Jesus was absolute in its core principles. It was not his human body or reasoning that made Jesus divine, but his (divine) will which was contained within the absolute will of God.

Jesus can be thought of as the absolute will of God, enveloped with created human attributes. Around his absolute core is

---

beginning and the end of all creation.

— "Jesus" is the man Jesus, who is now the pre-eminent individual of the person Christ. "Jesus of Nazareth" describes the human nature of Jesus. "Jesus Christ" describes the divine nature of Jesus. When Christ incarnates directly, Jesus results. When Christ incarnates indirectly, using his attributes to form nothing into something, humanity and all creation results.

— "God" is all that has absolute existence and being. It is impossible to become God, because God cannot be brought into being. However, God is free to include others into his person, and does this via Jesus who is the human nature of God.

— "Divine" refers to all who are fully included into the absolute being of God, via the body of Christ. This idea of divinization has been spoken of by the apostles and saints for 2000 years. The idea of our divinization is supported in catechism and scripture, (2Pet 1:4, 1Jn 3:2, Lk 6:40, 16:26; CCC 260, 398, 460, 795, 1988), St. John of the Cross also spoke of this idea. The book "Mystical Evolution" by Fr. John Arintero, is an extensive study of spiritual advancement from humanity to divinity and is still in print.

non-absolute flesh, emotions, awareness and reason. His human free will was free within the bounds of the divine will. Jesus is the human nature of the Son of God.[8]

The divine will of Jesus did not micromanage his human actions, rather he used his human will, which operated within the larger bounds of the divine will. Jesus' human will was used for human actions, while he had recourse to his divine, all powerful will in supernatural acts, to perform miracles for example. Likewise, the divine intellect of Jesus was used in prophetic knowledge, rather than in his work as a carpenter.

Christ is now the entire body of Christ. It is no longer a matter of one divine intellect and one human intellect. The entire body of Christ has millions of human minds and wills, not to mention its angelic members. We begin our participation in the body of Christ as a member of the human Christ. The human Christ is now the many fallible members who constitute the ***ongoing Christ*** on earth. We work toward perfection, in hope of one day sharing in the divine nature of God, (2Pet 1:4, 1Jn 3:2, Lk 6:40, 16:26; CCC 260, 460, 795, 1988).[9]

---

[8] The will of Jesus was divine and incorruptible. The human body and soul of Jesus was created like Adam, in that it was fully human but had no contact with sin and its corrupting effects. At the last supper, Jesus enlarged his person into the body of Christ, by including the apostles along with their sin. At this point the humanity of Jesus was corrupted and ended in death. His divine will remained incorruptible and mediated the apostle's sin into virtue, allowing their inclusion into his larger body of Christ.

[9] The destiny of every member of the body of Christ is divinization, (CCC 398). The human Jesus is no exception. Jesus (who is the human nature of God), is now fully divine. Jesus is now fully divine and has no contact with sin. The human nature of the Son of God is now the ongoing Christ on earth—that's us. God relies on the ongoing Christ to continue the redemptive mediation of sin into virtue, so that new members may be incorporated into the body of Christ. The one person of Christ is made of many individual members. Members each have a particular function, Jesus is the head directing the work of the members who now remediate sin into virtue. When the person of Christ (body of Christ) makes someone's sin into his virtue, that person now exists within Christ.

Our participation in the body of Christ is first in the human nature of Christ (which explains why we are not divine in this life), then finally in the divine person of Christ in Heaven. It is Catholic doctrine that the faithful are the literal person and body of Christ, (CCC 795, 789; 1Cor 12:27, Rm 12:5, 1Cor 1:2, 1Cor 6:15). The Catholic Church uses the term "mystical body of Christ", with mystical meaning mysterious, but not symbolic. The single person Christ is now all who are members of the body of Christ.

Jesus did not require salvation—that is membership in the body of Christ—because he was a member of the body of Christ at his creation. We in comparison, are *adopted* into the body of Christ.

In summary:

- The body of Christ is no longer Jesus alone, but all who constitute Christ, as the body of Christ.

- The human nature of Jesus was divinized, and the task of remediation of sin now falls on the *ongoing human Christ* on earth, that us. This enlarged body of Christ has perfected and divinized members in Heaven, while the ongoing human Christ on earth works toward this goal.

- Our initial membership in Christ is in this ongoing human Christ on earth. Jesus now awaits us in Heaven where we will be incorporated into his divine nature.

Body of Christ

By his own generous act, Christ is irreversibly all who participate in him.[10] Early Church writers coined the term "Whole Christ" to designate the entire body of Christ. The Whole Christ includes non-human members as well — angels, and the Eucharist.

---

[10] The Catechism of the Catholic Church states explicitly that we become Christ in at least two paragraphs: (1) CCC 1213, "Through baptism we are freed from sin and reborn as sons of God; we become members of Christ."; (2) CCC 795, "...Let us rejoice then and give thanks that we have become not only Christians, but Christ himself...he and we together are the whole man.". The idea and term "Whole Christ", occurs at least six times: CCC 795, 796, 797, 1136, 1187, 1188. Christ is now all who constitute the body of Christ: Jesus, Eucharist, humans, angels. This is not our presumptive desire, but God's own will for us.

Christ is the origin and end of all creation, the alpha and the omega, (Rev 22:13). We have our beginning as thought and will internal to Christ. We are given creation and a non-absolute free will. We are to cultivate ourselves into mature children of God. Sin was never intended, but our divine inclusion into Christ was the plan "from the foundations of the world", (CCC 398, Mt 25:34).

A literal understanding of our membership in the body of Christ, brings a new interpretation of the oft sited parable of the vineyard workers, (Mt 20: 1-16). This interpretation is not one of social justice, but the gift of divine participation. The same wage given to all is a sharing in the very life of God, which cannot be divided or given by degree. The same wage given to all workers is the absolute life of God which is not a matter of degree of greatness, but of absolute goodness.

The angels are members of the body of Christ, and not just helpful outsiders. We know that the angels underwent judgment. God intended communion with the angels just like his human children, (CCC 398).[11] This communion was made, but not all angels made it. The angels were now of two groups, those who "participated in the divine nature", (2Pet 1:4), and those who lived in corruption. See also the article on Hell in this appendix. The human Jesus did not then exist, and communion with the angels would have been made by the Trinitarian Son of God.

It is interesting to observe that Christ's communion with the angels makes Christianity as old as this first communion. The date for

---

11 ***CCC 398***, "...man was destined to be fully "divinized" by God in glory...". Even without sin, we were destined to rejoin Christ. Redemption of sin was not the original reason for Christ (since sin was never intended), communion was the reason. Sin was an unintended obstacle that Jesus Christ overcame, before he could make his originally intended communion with humanity.

2Pet 1:4, "...he has bestowed on us the precious and very great promises, so that through them you may come to share in the divine nature...".

Mt 25:34, "Then the king will say to those on his right, 'Come, you who are blessed by my Father. Inherit the kingdom prepared for you from the foundation of the world.'" As planned, God (Christ) intended us to go into creation and then return to his divine person.

Related verses for divinization: 2Pet 1:4, 1Jn 3:2, Lk 6:40, 16:26; CCC 260, 460, 795, 1988. Related verses for the faithful as the literal body of Christ: CCC 790, 795, 789; 1Cor 12:27, Rm 12:5, 1Cor 1:2, 1Cor 6:15.

Christianity is pushed back thousands of years prior to Jesus. We recall that Christianity at its core is communion into Christ.

We are certain that the angels were judged, with some not making their intended union with the divine Christ. The necessary conclusion is that other angels did make their intended union with Christ; this dates the formation of the extended body of Christ to a time earlier than the last supper, with the first communicants being the angels, rather than the apostles. Was St. Michael the archangel the first Pope of Christianity? Such an idea is not impossible if Christ appointed a leader angel.

Spirit

In both the canonical gospel and the Gospel of Thomas, Jesus often speaks of cause and effect, the soul and sin. These are all the consequences of moral decision, they are real spiritual happenings. Spirit is the "mechanism" as created by God by which creation operates. Events in creation are not a consequence of God pulling strings from Heaven, they are a consequence of humanity pushing levers on earth. These interconnecting levers are spirit: respect, moderation, reverence, love, hate. Just like matter, spirit is a creation of God. God is not a creation of the spirit world; rather, God creates and what he creates is first of all, spirit.

Spirit is intangible but as real as matter; and it has real effect. Spirit is immaterial being. Being is anything that exists: a rock, an idea, energy, emotion, logic, a person. Patience, respect, hate, reverence, morality, memory, free will are all spirit, and all have real effect in our world. Spirit is the underlying framework of all creation, and corruption of the willed moral virtues degrades the operation of all creation.

Spirit forms matter, spirit forms spirit, spirit forms events. *Consider that anything that can be described in terms of logic, will, virtue, act, emotion, mathematics or physical law has these same immaterial spirits or qualities as its foundation.* It is commonly known that energy and matter are the same substance in different configurations. Spirit, matter and events, likewise have an equivalence. Gospel accounts of this equivalence are the episodes in which Jesus makes bread, arms, legs (Mt 15:31), from nothing but his will; even events may be formed, the many biblical prophecies by

Jesus and others link moral action to distant future events. Immaterial acts are real, and have real effect in our world, beginning with ourselves. "Spiritual efficacy" is the principle of the real effect of spirit.[12]

Spirit by definition has no finite boundaries, will is the boundary for spirit—God's will, man's will. Because of moral free will, virtue may be corrupted into vice. ***God is not the origin of evil; abuse of virtue by moral beings is the origin of evil.*** Deviation from the original perfection of God's moral design necessarily causes disorder in our world. Any deviation from perfection can only be degradation.

We might observe that the material world is the real and normal order of creation, but before our material world existed, spirit alone was the medium of existence, (as with the community of the angels). This spiritual universe was no less real, and cause and effect were real within this spiritual realm. Indeed the world of matter is more like an overlay for the world of spirit. Spirit is the unseen framework of the entire universe, and was created as such by God. The practical consequences of this are that acts of patience, moderation, justice, generosity, chastity are real with real effects. The vices of these virtues are also real with real effect in our world. Spirit forms matter; spirit forms spirit; spirit forms events.

The idea that everything has a spirit is a necessary truth because everything has some immaterial qualities: logical or mathematical descriptions, willed moral virtues, time, emotion. Hundreds of years ago, St. Thomas Aquinas spoke of any *thing* having an underlying spirit that is mineral, vegetable or animal in nature. Disorder in our world is actually virtue which has become (partially) corrupted due to a lacking or misproportion. This corruption by misproportion comes about by willed mischoice by humanity.

We must give correct attention to God, ourselves and others in all our actions. If we fail in this, the resultant act is usually

---

[12] At a human societal level, most legal systems include the idea of moral infractions, (which are increasingly less enforced). The idea is that a person's character is the core from which his actions derive, it is his own personal spiritual framework, and no less real than body or property. Therefore an attempt to corrupt a person's morals is a type of assault on the real character, will and soul of that person. Harming the character of a person will result in harmful acts in the future. Ancient Israel took severe steps to remove such immaterial threats to their society, as commanded in the Law of Moses.

weighted towards self, at the expense of God or others. Sin is a misproportion of virtue, leaving a relative lacking of some virtue.

To take the quality of respect for example; we observe that when we give undue effort to self, dignity is corrupted into arrogance. If we fail to give proper moral effort to God, then irreverence results. If we fail to give others their due, then disrespect results.

In this example, if the student increased awareness of his own dignity, he would do well. But if he fails to also increase his efforts toward God's virtue of humility, then a relative lacking and resulting arrogance might result.

From this we see that moral corruption is a matter of lacking or deficit of what should be present. A lack of effort toward God leaves a relative predominance of self. The results are not theoretical, but take the forms of war, poverty, famine and disease.

Spirit interacts directly with spirit according to common elements. The biblical ideas of a family or a nation sharing in the effects of virtue or vice are examples. If a virtue is corrupted by a person of ancient Israel (to take a common biblical example), then all who share common virtues will suffer to some degree. Persons who are of the same: family, tribe, nation, world will all feel the effects of another's good of bad action.

This is the basis for the Biblical belief that children benefit or suffer from their parent's virtue or sin. It was true for Adam and Eve, and it is still true today. *This communal nature of spirit was created by God to benefit humanity,* but with the advent of the disorder of sin, disorder was shared in addition to goodness.

God's good judgment is also a factor by which spirit affects other spirit, matter or events. God is incapable of creating evil, but as our parent he does assign the evil of our sin to creation, according to his good judgment. In assigning the evil created by humanity, its disorder must be felt, but God could not assign evil with only an evil outcome possible.

A criticism of monotheism is that God seems to punish people by directing disorder (war, famine) upon them. In reality the evil of sin generated by humanity *must be effected within creation* (absolute divinity cannot be corrupted), God simply assigns our evil. God as our parent directs our evil according to his good judgment, for the highest goal — the salvation of souls. It is not a matter of God punishing our bad behavior, but of God assigning our disorder. This assignment may be made directly, or by extension, by the workings of nature for example. 1Cor 5:5 describes our evil being effected in this life, sparing condemnation in the next.

Just as goodness may be mediated into evil, evil may be mediated into goodness. It is a matter of anger being morally mediated into patience, greed mediated into moderation and trust, indifference into piety.

The human soul is a spirit; the soul is a "form", which gives function and purpose to one's body and actions. A human person might be thought of as a soul to which the property of physicality had been added. ***One's soul is the totality of one's immaterial attributes, and the operating principle of one's being***.

Animals are considered to have a soul (though not immortal as in humans), which governs their operations. The human soul has traditionally been partitioned into that part which governs moral activities (superior partition or spiritual soul), and that part which governs non-moral activities and the body, (inferior partition or material soul).

It is thought that the human soul is created by God using both direct and indirect means. Those faculties of the soul which govern the body are created at conception by biological means. Those faculties of the soul having a moral dimension are thought to be created directly by God.

The human soul is not static, but has the ability to "grow", and change. We may know our soul by observing our will, which in turn governs our thoughts and actions. Intellect, will and memory are properties of our soul.

Injustice and suffering in our world may only be truly eradicated by restoring its damaged spiritual foundation, which is the cause of evil. To give assistance after the fact is good, but even better is to prevent the disorder by avoiding those moral acts that degrade the spiritual foundations of our world and its people. This prevention is difficult to observe, because we are attempting to observe that which is prevented.

There is not a lack of good ideas in our world, but these do not take root in hearts because of moral disorder (sin) which corrupts will, faith, brotherhood and reasoning. War, hatred, greed and even disease, catastrophe and natural disasters are caused by the ongoing damage to the spiritual foundation of our world.

Hell

In the Gospel of Thomas, the idea of Heaven is more implicit, and the idea of Hell is more explicit. Heaven is full and perfected membership in Christ, who is now the entire body of Christ. Hell was never intended as a possibility, since sin was never a part of the plan. Hell is failure of (final) union in the body of Christ. Acting against the will of God in itself does not cast a person into Hell. Hell is an unintended by product of failed final communion.

Christ's plan never included sin, or even the need for salvation from Hell; what was planned was our divine communion with Christ, (CCC 398). Jesus Christ was to have made this communion with humanity, in the absence of sin. Christ came as planned, but first had to remediate sin before his communion with humanity. Jesus Christ did not incarnate because of sin, but in spite of sin according to God's original plan.

This communion occurred as planned, but now with the introduction of sin, Hell became a possibility. What we call judgment, is this originally intended divine communion with Christ. Death was never intended and this divine communion (CCC 398) was to have occurred in this life.[13]

---

[13] The intended sacrament for this communion was likely the Eucharist. Baptism inherently washes away sin, but sin was never a part of the plan, so Eucharist would have been the only planned sacrament for inclusion into the body of Christ. Both sacraments remediate sin and provide communion with Christ.

In the Eucharist Christ's purpose is to make communion, and in doing so remediates (venial) sin into virtue, in order to make the communion. In baptism Christ remediates our sin by making it into his own virtue, which also results in our communion with him.

Recall the last supper in which Jesus shared in the virtue and sin of the apostles by communion with them. That night at Gethsemane Jesus could not propagate or deflect this sin which was being presented to him, nor could he participate in the sin. The sin was presented to him by his human senses, emotions, and reason; his divine will reformed the apostles sin into his own virtue, thus providing union with himself.

In this communion, Christ takes goodness and those owning it, into himself. All evil and those owning it are unable to make union into Christ; what is left behind is evil (now devoid of all goodness), and those owning it. This is Hell.

Purgatory is membership in the body of Christ which is short of full divine union. Those in Purgatory participate in the human nature of Christ, but not yet in his full divine nature.

From this we see that Hell is a rejection of union with God, rather than God rejecting anyone. In fact Hell exists as a failure of final communion. God cannot make an act that has only an evil outcome, and condemning a person to Hell is an act with no possible final good. Hell as a punishment cannot be the design of God, it is an unintended result of failed final communion. This final communion is God's originally planned communion, now corrupted, (but not extinguished) by the evil of death.

Hell is produced by the condemned themselves and it occurs in two degrees. *The first degree of Hell* is internal to a soul, and occurs at judgment when that soul rejects and abandons God. The result of this willful separation is total *internal* corruption as goodness is abandoned. Catholic terminology for this first degree is the "particular judgment". The ***particular communion*** planned by God is now corrupted by sin into the particular judgement, and now with Hell as a possibility.

The second degree of Hell is yet to come. This is the general judgment when God unites with all goodness in creation, that "God may be all in all", (1Cor 15:28). God will take with him all the goodness abandoned by the reprobate, what remains will be evil, undiluted with goodness; this will be the final Hell. This Hell is what remains after God reclaims all goodness abandoned by angels and humanity.

The planned ***general communion*** is now the general judgment with Hell as a possibility. This general communion was Christ's desire to reunite and fulfill all of creation, that "God may be all in all", (1Cor 15:28). Everything comes from Christ, (Jn 1:3), and all is intended to rejoin Christ, even the lion who lies down with the lamb in divine Heaven.

Spiritual Advancement

In the Gospel of Thomas (and the canonical gospels), many abstruse teachings of Jesus are directed at spiritual advancement, which is a deeper sharing in the very person of Jesus Christ. This occurs as we eliminate self will, allowing a deeper indwelling of God's own spirit, the Holy Spirit. The Spirit is our likeness and union with God.

It sounds daunting and mystical, but it's no more mystical than living a just life as a first century carpenter. To deny one's self does not require abandoning family, food, sleep, or even the enjoyments of life, rather these are had according to God's will, not our own.

Personal spiritual advancement promotes social justice, and even salvation for others. We observe how original (and subsequent) sin introduced mistrust, greed, and hatred. These may be reformed by the mediation of spiritual advancement. When we suffer anger into patience, and greed into trust, individuals and nations are bettered, and the corruption is no longer suffered as social disorder.

The science of elimination of self is well developed; religious orders have for centuries molded their member's wills away from self, and toward God. These religious orders exist as practical aids to spiritual advancement, and their techniques may be used by anyone according to their circumstances. The seemingly pointless discipline they require has real results in mastering self will: uniforms, schedules, endless rules...there is little room for individual will. This selflessness becomes a habit, and over time a character of the soul. The sacraments they have received act with fuller effect, drawing them closer to God as self is mortified.

Conversely, our world is geared toward satisfaction, growth and indulgence of self...all to the detriment of our souls. We are told to eat richly, drink well, purchase, pleasure ourselves, get honor, find fault and demand our rights. Jesus had a different mindset. How would Jesus live if he were a reformed sinner, rich, bed ridden, a mother? Read the lives of the saints.

Purgative, Illuminative, Unitive ways

Jesus speaks, "The truest and most effective teaching that you can receive is this. Keep yourself apart from all men, if not in body, then in spirit. Keep yourself free from all unneeded images and words. Free yourself from everything that is accidental, binding or that brings worry. Always direct your spirit to the intimate contemplation of God, keeping me constantly present before your eyes and never turning them away from me. Direct all other exercises, be it poverty, fasting, vigils and all other types of chastisement toward this goal and make use of them to the extent that they advance this end."

"Do all this and you shall attain the summit of perfection that not one person in a thousand comprehends because they make these exercises their goal and therefore wander about for years."

This teaching of the prior two paragraphs, is known as "brief rules for spiritual advancement", given by Christ to St. Henry Suso. It is essentially a rephrasing of Christ's teaching in Mt 22:37, "You must love the Lord your God with all your heart, all your soul, and all your mind.". This phrasing by Jesus seems more attractive than the phrasing of the same idea, given to St. Suso. Suso's is perhaps more useful because of its detail.

Catholic teaching is of four afterlife states: Heaven, Hell, Purgatory, Limbo. 1Samuel 28:15 tells of the prophet Samuel in the afterlife of Limbo. With the coming of Christ, the holding area of Limbo was no longer needed, those able to entered Heaven, those needing purgation entered Purgatory. Limbo no longer seems to be operational.

To think of, and be Christ 24/7 sounds burdensome and impossible, but it's not. We do not become a first century carpenter, but a present day member of Christ, who is now the entire body of Christ: a mother, worker, student, unemployed, reforming sinner. We do not really have to learn more, or do more, or even be more. The less we cling to the accidents of this life, the deeper our participation in Christ. On the proactive side, the sacraments are essential, as they are the agents of our incorporation into Christ, as we clear the way of selfishness.

Spiritual advancement typically proceeds in stages and in a generally predictable pattern. Our efforts to free our soul of its illegitimate attachments is termed the Purgative way. Cultivation of virtue is the Illuminative way, and elimination of self for the purpose of union with Christ is the Unitive way. At any time our efforts are made predominantly, but not exclusively in one of these stages.

Our starting point depends on many factors, including the burden of original sin assigned to us; some have a greater burden to work through than others, (Luke 15:7). Most start their spiritual advancement in the Purgative way, and by repeated effort substantially eliminate sin from their lives.

The Illuminative stage is characterized by a virtuous and pious life, of legitimate undertakings in job, family, and all areas. The years of grinding perseverance have paid off for this person of virtue. Those courageously attaining the illuminative state, might expect a linear progression forward, but there is a necessary twist that occurs here, termed by St. John of the Cross "the dark night of the soul". It is almost always misunderstood by those entering into the Unitive stage, and may be a pitfall if not properly understood.

Spiritual trials now occur, by consent or initiative of God with the goal of eliminating the legitimate self will of the student. These trials are misunderstood as punishments, given for reasons that cannot even be determined. These trials feel like anything other than the blessing they are. To participate fully in Christ, we cannot stop at virtuous self; self must go, that we may become Christ.

An extreme example may be found in the book of Job. Job was scrupulous and perfect in his obedience to the decrees of God, and was richly rewarded. God sought to advance Job's soul by stripping him of his good fortune, leaving only faith in his life. He was to maintain faith and virtue, simply for the sake of God. Job had no part in sin, now he was tasked with eradicating even legitimate *self interest*. Job persevered and in the end he had no attachment, to this life, he fundamentally detached from it (Lk 14:26). His love of God was undiminished. Through this active and passive combination Job attained perfection...and his former joys were restored to him.

More commonly the casualty is not our material life as Job suffered, but our legitimate material and spiritual attachments. Until now the soul had attained conformity to God by degree, and now over an extended period may attain actual union with God—we become Christ.

Active and Passive Nights of the Soul

Another framework for this same process of spiritual advancement distinguishes sensual acts from spiritual acts, and active acts from passive acts. Overeating is a sensual act, while impure day dreams are spiritual acts. Active actions are undertakings of our own initiative. Passive actions originate from God, and are his act of deepening our inclusion into himself. St. John of the Cross first observed this four stage process of spiritual advancement. He wrote of it as literature, and not as a laid out system, because of this interpretations vary somewhat.

The pattern is: we rid our soul of sin and imperfection by our active moral efforts in both sensual and spiritual acts. As this is done we then advance in Christ passively, that is Christ takes the lead. This advancement is a deeper participation in his will and his very person, (CCC 789), and it's done by Christ, our part is simply to clear the way.

The sacraments are essential. Sacraments are Christ's instruments by which we advance, but sacraments cannot do their job unless they are allowed to.

In the *active night of the senses* the student takes the initiative in properly forming habits involving physical acts, drives and emotions. Habit is the key to one's character or one's soul, and reforming existing lesser habits involves repeated trial, error, and finally triumph. Not only must the illegitimate rule of the emotions be eliminated, but even legitimate emotions must be made subservient to the moral will.

The *passive night of the senses* occurs in parallel to the active night of the senses. As we actively free ourselves of sin, bad moral habits, pride and worry, we also advance in Christ in a passive manner. We see these former things as the chains that they are. We now share in Christ's own will and values. The sacraments bring this sharing in Christ, our part is making the moral effort. We clear a space for Christ in our soul.

Our emotions might be thought of as sense organs for our virtues. They react accordingly to virtue or corruption, proactively, or after the fact as in remorse. The proper place for emotions is under control of our will. Such control will not diminish joy, but help prefect it. Emotions are the primary driving force in many people, but the goal of Christian spiritual advancement is to attune our will to the perfect moral principles of Christ, rather than emotions.

In the *active night of the spirit*, the student takes the initiative in the proper formation of the moral will, and of faith. Our actions here are all actions with no material component: faith, love, patience, joy, imagination. These have little or no sensory component, but they are real acts with real effects, and there is a right way, a wrong way, and God's way to do each.

To this point, self (self is separation from God), has been presented disguised and as our own particular failings. In the advanced stages, the saints report unexpected feelings of abandonment, and dissatisfaction against God, (St. Faustina's diary, entry 77).

Sin is now presented to the student in its core form — rebellion against God. This undisguised rebellion may be presented alongside incomplete work from the previous stages, and our guide (in part) is our own imperfect soul, which we are trying to correct. Doing this cold turkey in a convent is easiest, but most people must take the home study curriculum.

We must forge ourselves into the Christ, and we do it on the cross. In the depths of the night of the spirit, the student feels abandoned, rejected, useless, sinful, purposeless, stupid. All this is unsatisfied self seeking, which must be mediated into good form and faith.

The turning point often occurs when the student finally sees the plan for him, and submits. All along has been the unfelt *passive night of the spirit*, but now it predominates. The trials are no longer meaningless, but purposeful, and the student finally joins in and rapid progress may be made. Near the end, God takes command. The student has largely gone as far as he can. God proceeds to strip away the last remnants of self, for the purpose of divine union.

The Divine union is the final stage of our existence within the body of Christ. This is the wedding feast that Jesus spoke of. It is the spiritual marriage that the saints participate in. It is our divinization and it was intended to occur in this life on earth.

Miracles, prophecy, ecstatic contemplation are all common in the divine union. The divinized student now has the unlimited ability of the divine Christ, the student is the divine Christ.

The divine union may be achieved in this life. It occurs when every attribute under willful control is free of disorder, this allows the willful whole to be incorporated into the divine Christ. The body, which is not fully under our willful control undergoes death. The Divine doctor himself conducts this soul transplant as the final stage of the passive night of the spirit.

This divine union on earth was the original plan for humanity, and everyone was to have attained it in this life. No afterlife was even planned; just a perfected, divine continuation of our current existence. Day trips to Heaven to visit the angels would be allowed, but Jesus would not have died on the cross, and we would all know him here on earth. Our world would have been a sort of spiritual utopia, with perfected, divinized elders (no wrinkles or arthritis) leading the upcoming generations to their intended divinization.

For our spiritual advancement, we might construct a three stage program, which we repeat until holy:

(1.) We identify and examine the problem and our foolish attachment to it. We do this in both structured mediation and on our feet as we encounter problems. We hold the temptation at arm's length to break the emotional cycle which feeds itself. This emotional cycle usually proceeds away from perfection and towards self: pity, indulgence, destruction.

We recall our goal (incorporation into Christ) and our reasons. We compare our proposed action to the person Christ, and not only the first century Christ, but the present day Christ: the mother, the worker, the person at leisure, danger or trouble. We think of our past failings in which we fail at the peak of temptation, only to kick ourselves later.

(2.) We ride out the peak and steamroll to virtue on the downside. We do not worry about the consequences, God will arrange those. We maintain focus on the only thing that lasts or has value, our participation in Christ.

(3.) Cultivation of peace is the next (and necessary) event. We must not eliminate vice, pride and worry, only to complain of boredom. Our calling is to express ourselves as Christ in the many ways open to us. Christ seeks to express himself in every legitimate art or enterprise, and "non-religious" acts are not less than religious acts. Indeed, to carve out a part of life for religion, implies that the other part does not seek inclusion into God. In ancient Israel there was no divide (in theory) between God, government, business, family. They were all God's enterprises under our stewardship. With the advent of Christianity, we are not stewards for Christ, but Christ himself, and this life is our productive training ground.

Spiritual advancement is not so different from quitting: smoking, overeating, addiction, pornography, depression, and other imperfections.[14] In fact conquering any of these things or others is spiritual advancement. In redirecting our will from one self centered habit to another ideal derived habit we break the hump and cultivate the habit. Again, we repeat until holy. This is what every saint has done, and we are called to divine perfection in this life.

Not just temptation to sin, but decisions also should be given this program of scrutiny. A good decision may be made better by it, and we advance as Christ. Idle thoughts are not so idle, (Mt 5:28). We can and should practice the best possible thought. This is the core value of prayer, it is proactive good thought and will which has great meaning for eternity.

The ten commandments are in order of importance. God comes first; separation from God only brings a corresponding separation from God's good design for our world. Praise of God implies an association of wills with God. Positive prayer joined to acts of selflessness advance our incorporation into God, and our families

---

[14] In the case of genetic or chemical predisposition to any imperfection, we cannot (short of miraculous intervention), stop the disposition, because our chemistry is not really under our willful control. However, our <u>will</u> may be developed stronger than our imperfections. The imperfection is controlled, rather it controlling us. The saints have conquered every sort and degree of imperfection, and so can we. As the body of Christ, we need not rely only on our mere human strength, we have the entirety of Christ to help us.

and the world benefit. Lack of external resources does not prohibit great influence in our world.

Spiritual advancement is not primarily a matter of reading or study, but of doing and not doing. Most who have made the effort (and were literate) used only the Gospel and the Holy Spirit as guides. Confirmation is the sacrament for spiritual advancement, and adult evening classes are available.

______________ooOoo______________

Consider giving a copy of this book to your priest or bishop. Theology of other dimensions of the Catholic faith such as Euchrist, BVM, Purgatory, and more, may be read in the author's book, "A Maximum Understanding of the Body of Christ". In paperback or free online.